HOUSES OF BRITAIN
the outside view

The new edition

Since my father wrote this book a lot has happened to the built landscape of the British Isles. Twice as much land as was built over in 1975 has been built over now, the economy has put money into the repair and modernisation of most of the existing housing stock. The traditional has been aped but only in the manner that it always has been and it is the intention of this book to communicate the intentions of the maker or designer of a house and the appropriate manner in which to work with a house by being sympathetic to it.

It is amazing the way someone who can restore a classic car to a condition slightly better than when it left the factory has no such respect for the similar design values of their house. Of course living in an old house involves adding to its history but you are only looking after it for the future and don't really own it as much as say owning a Rembrandt would entitle you to alter it.

Metric measures are now shown after imperial because practically all of the buildings shown in this book would have been designed, specified and built using imperial measurements and proportions.

Mark Pinglan   2003

The Blue Circle Group, who have always promoted the judicious use of colour for buildings, have commissioned and sponsored this book. In no other way would it have been possible to undertake the vast amount of research and design work, spread over more than three years, and resulting in the exquisite scaled drawings and photographs which make this book not only a unique work of practical reference but a very timely contribution to Britain's architectural heritage.

HOUSES OF BRITAIN
the outside view

John Prizeman
Foreword by The Duke of Gloucester

Quiller Press

Published by
Quiller Press Ltd.,
46 Lillie Road,
London, SW6 ITN

First published as Your House - the Outside View 1975,
new edition 1982
First published this edition 2003

© 1974 Blue Circle Industries PLC and 2003 Mark Prizeman
Printed through Colorcraft Ltd, Hong Kong

ISBN 1 899163 67 0

The quotations on the jacket, are taken from reviews of the
book when it was originally published in 1975 under the
title *Your House – the Outside View.*

The drawings are all to a scale of 1:150. As far
as possible the houses have been shown as
4 originally designed.

Contents

7   Foreword

8   Introduction

10 Sources of information

12 Colour appreciation

24 Colour history

28 Colours for houses

40 Design influences

42 Building in timber

54 Building in mud

60 Building in stone

80 Building in brick

96 Rendering

102 Modern methods

106 Chimneys, roofs and gutters

112 Walls

116 Doors and windows

120 Paving, paths and boundaries

122 Conservatories, garages and other extensions

128 Protective treatments

132 Further reading

133 Museums

133 Acknowledgements

134 Index

Contributors

ART DIRECTION
Alan Keeler

RESEARCH
Joanna Tanlaw

DRAWINGS
Roy Castle
Brian Craker
Alan Keeler
Don Kidman
Stanley Paine
Marjorie Saynor

PHOTOGRAPHS
Willow Bentley
Peter Grondona
Alan Keeler
Don Kidman
Lucinda Lambton
Dewhurst Macfarlane
James Mortimer
Neil Nimmo
John Prizeman
Mark Prizeman
Eddie Ryle-Hodges
Joanna Tanlaw

TYPOGRAPHY
Trudy Temkin

Foreword to the new edition
The Duke of Gloucester KG GCVO

Blenheim Palace or Hampton Court are best described in the language of the art historian whereas the average semi-detached house is normally only considered in the jargon of the estate agent. The author of this book succeeds in bridging this enormous gap. It is not his intention to prove that all houses are works of art, but rather that they all have an intrinsic character of their own, which must be recognised, either because of the particular building technique employed, or because of some architectural effect consciously intended. I agree wholeheartedly with the principal message of the book that to ignore this special character, whatever it may happen to be, and to apply an opposing architectural intention, is to risk making the house look ridiculous and possibly quite inappropriate. After all nobody's fooled if you put a Rolls Royce bonnet on a mini.

To save the house owner from falling into this trap, the author takes a wide range of house types from every region and every period, and gives a rational explanation of why they appear the way that they do.

The book was originally entitled Your House because the range of house types is so large that there is almost bound to be one similar to your own and this example, taken together with the general advice found in later sections of the book, should be of great assistance to those who are contemplating altering the appearance of their house.

Not only does this book describe "your house" but inevitably many others as well. Our attitude to other people's houses varies from toleration towards a necessary evil that we tend to ignore, to admiration for houses in places that attract tourists like Bath or Lavenham. John Prizeman shows how many houses could be restored and how a coat of paint of the right colour can revive many a run-down façade, but he also shows us how to appreciate many kinds of houses for their own sake.

For every tourist who has paid to see a stately home there must be a great number of others who have enjoyed wandering around a town or village and appreciated the architecture and the atmosphere for free.

This book should be of great help to those who like to look for themselves and of encouragement to those who are in a position to make their own contribution to the quality of our environment.

January 2003

7

Introduction

THE FACE OF A HOUSE is the face of the man it was built for: it shows his character, tastes, interests, wealth, fears and aspirations more clearly than anything he may say about himself. The face of a house also reflects the climate, geology, craftsmanship, materials, fashions and building laws current when it was built: the face of history, easily examined without the use of a time machine. To destroy or change the face of a house is to lose or alter exact evidence of the past. This is not to suggest that we should live in museums, but far more people live in old houses than new and this book is about understanding why houses look the way they do and how we may care for them.

The idea for the book came while driving through streets of 20th-century houses in South London, a continuous parade of all the various influences which have inspired British house building through the centuries. Anglo-Saxon half-timber and thatch, Norman arches, Dutch gables, French Gothic, Italian villa, German Bauhaus, Swedish modern, none by any means exact copies but each reflecting the builder's view of what was appropriate for the time. Purists will call these fantasies, but that is the biggest fantasy of all: houses, however humble, have always managed to have something unnecessary from the purely materialistic view but essential for the spirit and a sense of humour.

Each week in the salerooms old pictures and furniture make record prices. Very often at the same time the houses which once held those articles are either being knocked down or visually mutilated by inept modernisation. It is curious that while we carefully clean, renovate and restore pictures and furniture to their original state, we rarely do the same for our buildings. Houses are valued for their usefulness and for their position and only rarely for their design, yet the design of a house is just as much a reflection of the society which built it as its contents. It is even odder when it is considered that most valued objects from the past are either useless for their original purpose (old clocks, telescopes, coffee grinders) or too precious for daily use (old glass, china, silver). Every house was once someone's dream of home, even if only a developer's dream home to sell to someone else. Like people, houses are not created in a vacuum; their design has always been influenced by that of many previous houses. The much maligned Tudor-style semi-detached has a perfectly respectable lineage dating back through the craft movement of the late 19th century, the romantic cottages of John Nash at the beginning of that century, through the rustic designs of the 18th century to the simple farmhouses of the 16th and 17th centuries and back to the 14th- and 15th-century manor houses. They did not just happen but are an expression of the pleasure to be found in the romantic mixture of timber, plaster, lead and brickwork. The desire for precision and conformity is reflected in the parallel development of the neo-Georgian house which can be traced back through the Queen Anne revival at the end of the 19th century, through the continuous development of the classical terrace from about 1700 onwards, to the individual Palladian-style country houses of the 17th century and the exact symmetry of Elizabethan houses and earlier. The older a house is the more likely it is to have been altered from its original design, often in the most dramatic way. Already it is quite difficult to find 1930s houses which have not had a modern front door put in, a picture window added or the original crazy paving replaced with variegated coloured slabs. Although no-one would dream of replacing the windows in a Canaletto painting of London with modern picture windows or repainting the thatch of a Constable cottage with machine-made tiles and spotting in coach lamps by the door, this is just what is happening all the time everywhere to real houses. Misguided affluence is second only to neglect as the greatest danger to the visual quality of our homes.

All over the British Isles there are beautiful Georgian houses used as storerooms, often only the top windows retaining the original window bars, with single-storey shops built over the front garden – the kind of property that planning authorities (not all of whom are the most visually aware of bodies) will often allow to be pulled down without realising that it is like tearing up a Reynolds. Under the dirt and grime and the thoughtless revisions of later owners many houses have a hidden asset well worth restoring – an asset which may indeed add to the value of the property and which will certainly add a great deal of enjoyment to the occupiers and to anyone passing by.

There are a few simple guides. Above all, it is dangerous to try and make a house into something which it is not. All that is needed is an affectionate respect for the ideas and workmanship of the original.

1 This terrace, apparently of Victorian shops, was originally a row of Georgian houses (the one on the right still has its correct upper windows) and is typical of many that were altered in the 19th century to suit the taste of the time. Their true quality, like that of many old paintings, will only be seen after careful restoration.

2 A small square surrounded by tiny cottages (built at a time when people were much shorter) has been dwarfed by its use as a car park, when it could have given pleasure as a pedestrian square with a few trees and benches. Many similar groups of convenient little houses around our old city centres have even been demolished to make room for cars.

3 A cross-roads in a small Devon town. The church tower amidst a group of stone village houses, with a steeply curving hillside behind, should have made an interesting picture. A combination of acres of asphalt, complicated road signs, inept positioning of lamp posts, serves to prevent a true appreciation of the view. The pathetic little row of flowers underlines the lack of visual awareness displayed by the authorities.

1

2

3

4

5

4 This elegant Regency house, passed over by Planning Authorities who did not recognise its quality has now been demolished to make way for new housing.

5 This minor road in a Cambridgeshire village has a number of old thatched cottages. The enormous bleak lamp-posts badly positioned are a rude affront.

Sources of information

BEFORE GOING to one of the many organisations or professions for help and advice, try and find out as much as possible about the history of your house. The local public library is a good place to start: there is normally an historical section with building records where you can find the date of construction and the name of the architect and builder. The planning authority may also be helpful; there is usually at least one person, if not a department, whose job it is to advise on the architectural merit of the buildings in the area. If the house was built recently they will have copies of the drawings, as will the department dealing with building regulations.

A house has some history however recently it was built: who designed it, who built it, for whom it was built, who has lived in it, and the materials it is made from all make up a story. Architects work longer than other professionals and during their lifetime usually have a hand in an enormous number of buildings. Although relatively few houses are the personal work of an architect who has designed and supervised every detail, most were built to plans originally drawn by an architect who may be more or less famous. 18th- and 19th-century houses were often built to designs from pattern books written by well-known architects and these, though now rare, can be found in reference libraries. The builder and developer, often one firm, can have a long local history and a particular house they have built will have a position in a steadily developing design story that alters as tastes and needs changed. The life-style of the original owner will have had a great deal to do with the design of the house.

A common problem is fitting the relaxed weekender into a cottage originally designed for a hard-working farm labourer, but an understanding of the way he lived is helpful. The search for new and quicker means of building has meant that many houses built in the last hundred years or so use interesting constructional methods, though covered by a conventional exterior.

In theory professional advice, although seemingly expensive, should save time and money overall; in practice it will only do so if you choose the right firm. Time spent in deciding exactly what advice you want and then choosing someone who is best able to give that advice is never wasted. If you want advice on improving the visual appearance of the house, choose an architect or designer who has a sense of history and a good eye for colour. They will advise on design faults which need correcting; for instance, Georgian window bars that need replacing, a better place for the TV aerial, the kind of planting, fences and paving that would look well. They can produce a series of drawings showing different ways in which the house can be coloured with a firm recommendation for the one they like best. This advice need not cost very much; it is the product of skill and experience, takes little professional time and should be enjoyed by all parties.

Construction faults, rising damp, rot, leaking roofs need a different kind of professional advice that takes much longer and can cost a great deal more. Some architects and surveyors specialise in the renovation of old buildings and they will advise on whether a structural engineer is also needed. They will know the best firms to go to or the best local craftsman. Renovating budgets can be very expensive but should be kept in perspective. Whereas a leaking roof must be attended to at once, a flaking stone wall or an old settlement crack that is no longer moving can be left until money is available, or even left altogether as part of the patina of time.

It is always useful to have a professional eye run over the house; sometimes the advice may simply be to go to a reputable firm that gives a free survey and estimate if the problem is limited to rising damp or rot. Employing a landscape architect may sound a little grand, but for a small house the charge is modest and the right firm will have an intimate knowledge of the problems posed by appropriate design, children, cars, animals and the cost of upkeep.

Successive governments have become increasingly aware of the value of our houses, not only as places to live in but also as part of our visual environment. For this reason a grading system has been in use since 1944 so that owners and local authorities can have some idea of the value of a particular house judged from a national point of view. Since 1970 houses have not only been graded individually but also as part of a group. Grants from local authorities, national Heritage groups and also some private charities are available and advice on these can be sought both from professionals and the local authority. It is a help if your house is listed or in a conservation area; but if not, remember the list is constantly being expanded and you can apply to be considered for grading or for your area to be. On the next page is a list of helpful organisations. Local planning authorities are generally very helpful.

1 Government services

Building Research Establishment Ltd.
Bucknalls Lane
Garston
Watford WD2 7JR
Tel: 01923 664000
www.bre.co.uk
Will answer technical queries on building construction problems

English Heritage
Customer Services Department
PO Box 569
Swindon SN2 2YP
Tel: 0870 333 1181
www.english-heritage.org.uk/sitemap/index.asp
www.englishheritage.org.uk
Gives grants for repairs to buildings of outstanding historical or architectural interest in England.

Historic Scotland
Longmore House
Salisbury Place
Edinburgh EH9 1SH
Tel: 0131 668 8800
www.historic-scotland.gov.uk/sw-frame.htm
Gives grants for repairs to buildings of outstanding historical or architectural interest in Scotland.

Cadw: Welsh Historic Monuments
National Assembly for Wales
Cathays Park
Cardiff CF10 3NQ
Tel: 029 2050 0200
www.cadw.wales.gov.uk
Recommends grants for repairs to buildings of outstanding historical or architectural interest in Wales.

National Monuments Record Centre
Kemble Drive
Swindon
Wiltshire SN2 2GZ
Tel: 01793 414 600
www.english-heritage.org.uk/knowledge/nmr
Compiles detailed records of ancient and historical monuments in England. Architectural records, library, photographs and drawings.

National Monument Record London Search Room
55 Blandford Street
London W1H 3HS
Tel: 020 7208 8200
www.english-heritage.org.uk/knowledge/nmr
Compiles detailed records of ancient and historical monuments in London. Houses the Survey of London.

Royal Commission on Ancient and Historical Monuments of Scotland
John Sinclair House
16 Bernard Terrace
Edinburgh EH8 9NX
Tel: 0131 662 1456
www.rcahms.gov.uk
Compiles detailed records of ancient and historical monuments in Scotland

Royal Commission on Ancient and Historical Monuments for Wales
Crown Building
Plas Crug
Aberystwyth SY23 2HP
www.rcahmw.org.uk
Compiles detailed records of ancient and historical monuments and antiquities in Wales.

2 Preservation groups

Ancient Monuments Society
St. Ann's Vestry Hall
2 Church Entry
London EC4V 5HB
Tel: 0207 236 3934
www.ancientmonumentssociety.org.uk
Studies and conserves ancient monuments, historic buildings and fine old craftsmanship

Society for the Protection of Ancient Buildings
37 Spital Square
London E1 6DY
Tel: 0207 377 1644
www.spab.org.uk
Advises on the treatment and repair of old buildings and their preservation.

The Georgian Group
6 Fitzroy Square
London W1P 6DX
Tel: 020 7387 1720
www. heritage.co.uk/georgian
Architectural conservation; advises on preservation and repair of Georgian buildings

Irish Georgian Society
74 Merrion Square
Dublin 2
Eire
Tel: 00 353 1 676 7053
www. irish-architecture.com/igs
www. irishgeorgiansociety.org
Protects Irish architecture, records Irish buildings.

Architectural Heritage Society of Scotland
The Glasite Meeting House
33 Barony Street
Edinburgh EH3 6NX
Tel: 01 31 557 0019
www.ahss.org.uk
Protects Scottish architecture and records Scottish buildings.

Victorian Society
1 Priory Gardens
Bedford Park
London W4 1TT
Tel: 020 8994 1019
www.victorian-society.org.uk
Records and protects Victorian and Edwardian buildings.

The Twentieth Century Society
70 Cowcross Street
London EC1M 6EJ
Tel: 020 7250 3857
www.c20society.demon.co.uk
Records and protects twentieth century buildings.

Campaign for the Protection of Rural England
Warwick House
25 Buckingham Palace Road
London SW1W OPP
Tel: 020 7976 6433
www.cpre.org.uk
Protects rural landscape and buildings, including country towns and houses in England.

Campaign for the Protection of Rural Wales
Ymgyrch Diogelu Cymru Wledig
Ty Gwyn
31 High Street
Welshpool
Powys SY21 7JP
Tel: 01938 55 2525
www.cprw.org.uk
Protects rural landscape and buildings, including country towns and houses in Wales.

The Association for the Protection of Rural Scotland
Gladstone's Land (3rd Floor)
483 Lawnmarket
Edinburgh EH1 2NT
Tel: 0131 225 7012
www.aprs.org.uk
Protects rural landscape and buildings, including country towns and houses in Scotland.

3 General references

The British Library at St Pancras
96 Euston Road
London NW1 2DB
Tel: 020 7412 7000
www.bl.uk
Useful reference for source books and drawings of houses of all periods.

Sir John Soane's Museum
13 Lincoln's Inn Fields
London WC2A 3BP
Tel: 020 7405 2107
www.soane.org
Useful reference for source books and drawings of houses particularly of the classical period.

The Crafts Council
44a Pentonville Road
London N1 9BY
Tel: 020 7589 4090
www.craftscouncil.org.uk
Has an index of all craftsmen in England and Wales.

RIBA Drawings collection
21 Portman Square
London W1H 9HF
Tel: 020 7580 5533
www.site.yahoo.net/riba-library/drawcol.html
Collection of architectural drawings, shortly moving to the V&A museum.

British Geological Survey
Kingsley Dunham Centre
Keyworth
Nottingham NG12 5GG
Tel: +44 (0)115 936 3100

British Geological Survey
London Information Office
Natural History Museum
Earth Galleries
Exhibition Road
London SW7 2DE
Tel: 020 7589 4090
www.bgs.ac.uk
Will identify stones and advise on where to get them.

Local Libraries and Local Authorities

Colour appreciation

A RAY OF SUNSHINE at midday seems to be white light unless we see it refracted by a shower of rain, when it appears as all the colours of the rainbow. It also contains other kinds of ray: heat, ultra-violet, radio and X-rays. Their effect depends upon their rate of vibration: the rays we see by are only about one-fifteenth of the total produced by the sun and, if the universe is included, about one-sixtieth. They occur about midway in the whole range between heat and ultra violet and within the group each colour has its own rate of vibration ranging from the slowest, red, through orange, yellow, green, blue to violet vibrating twice as fast as red. Compared with sound, red corresponds to a low note, violet to a high one. All these rays contain energy and the force of their impact can be physically measured. Colour rays are seen when anything becomes sufficiently hot to make it glow, like the sun or a red-hot poker or the filament in a light bulb; different materials and different temperatures give different selections of colour rays. Colour rays are only seen when they are reflected off something – in the case of sunrays, dust particles in the atmosphere – or when looking directly at the source such as the sun itself. Colour has no existence except in the brain. It is produced by the effect of the rays measured by the eye and transferred to the brain, so it can be argued that an uninhabited island has no colour; it must be seen before it can exist. Although birds, fish, reptiles and insects like bees have a highly developed colour sense, only man and his close relations such as apes and monkeys have colour vision. Dogs and cats live in a grey world and bulls cannot actually see red.

Since white light is not just one ray but a whole collection it can be selectively broken up by different materials. When white light strikes a material, a little is reflected from the surface, but the rest passes below, where the different rays are either absorbed or rejected. We call the colour of the object the colour of the reflected rays. Yellow paint absorbs all the colour rays except yellow and a little green. Blue paint absorbs all but blue and a little green. Mix the two together and we see green, because it is the only colour they both reflect. If all the rays absorbed are reflected the material appears white, but if none is reflected it appears black. The same will happen to adjacent heat waves, which is why in the sun white is cooler than black. If all the rays pass through, the material will appear transparent but it will slow down the rays by varying amounts, depending on their speed of vibration. This is why, when they pass at an angle into and are reflected out of rain-drops, they form a rainbow, since each colour as it slows is bent at a different angle, the slowest – red – least, the fastest – violet – most. In this way the original white light is split into its components. If the light is almost entirely reflected from the surface it will appear gold or silver depending on the amount of colour absorbed; if all the light is reflected the surface appears as a mirror.

The reflected colours from an object in view are absorbed by three kinds of receptor sensitive to red, green and blue at the back of the eye. Although white light contains all the rainbow colours, a combination of red, blue and green (the primary colours for light) will also produce white light and mixtures of these will produce most of the others. It is a puzzle for anyone who has mixed red and green paint to make muddy black, to find that green and red lights make yellow, until it is realised that the lights are adding colours and thus the more colours there are, the whiter the light becomes. The more coloured paints are mixed together, the blacker they become, because between them they steadily absorb all the coloured rays: only the colours common to all can be reflected and seen. The primary colours are red, yellow and blue.

The combined responses from the receptors in the eye inform the brain what colour it should see, although colours are not only produced by the eye – for instance, they also occur in dreams. The green and red receptors are more sensitive than the blue, so any variation in the combination of these two – yellow – is easily detected. As a result yellow, which occurs about the middle of the colour range, is the most easily seen of colours. Subtle shades of blue, red and violet are much less easily distinguished.

Not all colours seen can be resolved from white light; brown, purple, gold, silver, copper are registered in the brain through complicated interactions between the receptors in the eye. Not all light is white; even during the day the sun's light is changing colour because, as the sun rises or falls, it has to pass through varying depths of atmosphere containing dust which absorbs some of its colours.

Colour-blindness occurs when the messages from one or more of the receptors in the eye are defective. Red and green are most commonly confused. It is very rare in women but affects 5 per cent to 10 per cent of men. With normal sight everyone sees the same colour, though the intensity can vary with age and health. The reason that different responses are made by individuals to the same colour is because of past associations and experiences stored in the brain, so children have a much fresher approach to colour than most adults. The classic example of the brain adjusting the information it receives is a white tablecloth in candlelight. The adult will see it as white because of previous knowledge. A child is most likely to see it as yellow because that is the colour the candlelight has given it. An orange sphere will actually look more orange when it is known that it really is orange. Tungsten or even candle light looks white enough until colours seen by them are compared in daylight. The brain sees white because it thinks it should be seeing white. Because the brain associates colours with previous experiences, they create different emotional responses. For instance, blue feels cool and expansive through association with water and sky. It is a colour most men prefer, whatever they say about blondes. Red feels warm and close, reminding the brain of fire and blood; it is the first colour a baby distinguishes and the first colour to be named in primitive languages. It is also the colour preferred by most women. Since colour rays have energy they also have temperatures, and red is in fact physically warmer than blue. Red light raises the pulse and blood pressure: blue light has the opposite effect. Some colours, like clear yellow, associated with sunshine, are generally liked, whereas brown yellows are not, since they are associated with dirt and disease.

The eye is much less sensitive than the ear and is easily confused. Colour design must take account both of the possibility of confusion as well as the psychological responses added by the brain. Because the eye tires when it looks at one colour for more than about thirty seconds, the particular receptor ceases to function fully and the eye will prefer a change to the opposite colour, so that it can use the other receptors. As an experiment, look at a patch of any bright colour for half a minute and then at a white sheet of paper. The shape of the bright colour will appear, but the colour will be its opposite. These colours are called complementary – mixed as paints they make black, as lights they make white. Placed side by side, the eye can see them more clearly than any other combination, so they both appear enhanced. Orange and blue are complementary; placed

together, the blue will seem bluer, the orange more orange. To help it to see more clearly, the eye will surround the colour it is looking at with a little halo of the complementary colour, so altering the adjacent colour. Grey will therefore seem greenish next to red, reddish next to green. For the same reason the eye will accentuate differences between colours: green surrounded by yellow will appear cooler than the same green surrounded by blue, which will make it seem warmer than it really is. A large patch of bright colour will swamp a small patch of dull colour, making it difficult to see clearly. The converse is true of a small patch of bright colour in a large area of dull; it will show up clearly.

Normally we like to feel secure, especially concerning anything to do with the home. Although strange and exciting emotions can be created by disturbing the brain with colour combinations that are difficult for it to deal with, the history of exterior decoration has one rule for success; clarity of perception. Colour schemes that contrast, like the traditional black-and-white house decoration of Cumbria, or are complementary, like the frequently seen green woodwork on a red-brick house, are most often used. Colours which together have some similarity, making them sympathetic perhaps because they are the same tone in terms of light and dark, and thus easy on the eye, are another group. Slate-roofed redbrick houses are a good example. Many buildings rely on monochrome for their effect, like the great variety of different shades of buff in a Cotswold stone village.

The problem of how to measure colour in practical terms was solved, at least for the paint industry, by the American portrait painter, Albert H. Munsell. He first published his *Atlas of the Color System* in 1915 with its system of notation that enables most colours to be defined. Other methods of colour measurement are now used but the Munsell system remains the most important. What is normally loosely called 'colour' is defined by three qualities: Hue, Value and Chroma. Hue describes whether the sample in question is red, blue, green or whatever. The brain, by adding purple to the colours of the rainbow, added the missing link between dark red and violet, allowing colours to be thought of as a continuous circle of graduating hues. Munsell divided this circle into ten main hues: Red, Yellow Red, Yellow, Green Yellow and so on until he was back to Purple, Red Purple and Red. Each main hue is divid-

ed on the circle into a further ten divisions which grade it from the previous hue on to the next. Each of these can be further subdivided by ten and so on, so that the finest gradation of hue can be described numerically. Pure red, for instance, is called 5R. Halfway to yellow red, it becomes 10R, and a fine gradation between might be called 8.75R.

The second way in which colours can be described is by their lightness or darkness. Taking the centre of the circle as neutral, without colour in terms of hue, Munsell extended this vertically from black to white, dividing it into ten visually equal subdivisions. These could be infinitely subdivided by decimal breakdown. This quality of colour measurement he called Value and it is directly related to the amount of light reflected. The neutral colours in the centre can only be described by their value number: a medium grey is called N5, a very pale grey N9. For colours with hue, Munsell added the appropriate value number, so a middle shade of red might be 5R 5.

Munsell called the amount of colour in a hue, Chroma. He could then describe for a particular hue of red the variations from palest pink to brightest pink by a further set of numbers extending from zero by steps of equal visual importance to about twenty for the strongest-coloured specimens producible. As in hue, fine gradations could be described by decimal subdivision. Taking the centre of Munsell's hue circle as having no colour – zero – each chroma subdivision becomes more intense towards the perimeter. A brightly coloured middle shade of red could be written 5R 5/14. Although the Munsell system is infinitely precise, in practice it is only possible to visually differentiate between 200 hues around the circle, 100 value steps and about 50 degrees of chroma. This gives the possibility of visually differentiating between one million colours. The Munsell atlas is available through public libraries (it is very expensive to buy) and contains 1,500 colour samples.

There remains the problem of explaining good colours and good colour combinations. They are those that please and satisfy through all the vastly complicated mechanisms of eye and brain. They can be recognised by the tranquillity they give; a sense that no alteration could improve their quality or harmony. But the mind is easily bored and, as in music a once-loved tune becomes sickening after too much repetition, so popular colours and colour combinations are constantly changing.

The house in the landscape (*Mid-Wales*)
Any building in an open landscape becomes a visual focal point because it is something we immediately identify with: a man-made structure against a natural background. When it is logically situated, a house can vastly enhance a view, especially if it is designed and coloured in a manner sympathetic to the area. The siting of a house in the past had overriding considerations that today are of little or no importance. Health was the most important of all in times when medical services were poor: the Roman superstition that success in future events could be foretold by examining the entrails of animals was based on the sensible habit of studying local animal life to see if it was healthy, before choosing a building site. If the animals were healthy, then the chances

were that humans would be too. Medieval houses in the British Isles faced north or east so that the sun could not liven up the filthy rush flooring of the time. When rushes were abandoned, homes could face the sunny south. Victorian books on house building include long sections on how to choose a healthy site and estate agents still used health as a sales point well into the 1920s.

Piped water and main drainage allow houses to be built practically anywhere, but in the past houses were only built where there was good water near at hand from either a well or a spring and ideally with a good slope of land for drainage and a porous soil. Good soil was also needed for growing the medicinal and culinary herbs essential to the household, as well as fruit, vegetables and small crops. Every locality

has its own small variations in climate: one side of a hill is drier than the other, one faces the prevailing wind, another forms a frost pocket. Local knowledge was always available for choosing the best place to live. Only rarely did considerations of defence affect building sites, usually limited in post-medieval times to coasts visited by pirates, like Devon and Cornwall and border areas. The pleasures to be found in a good view have only been recognised since classical design was introduced in the 17th century and it is only in our own claustrophobic times that a good view has become a desirable priority.

The logical reasons for siting houses have resulted in sites being used many times over, often since prehistory; with the result that we instinctively respond to them.

The house in the townscape (*Scotland*)

Houses in a town, like trees in a wood, cease to be individual units and become part of a whole. In a medieval street, or a row of simple cottages, it is difficult to see where one house finishes and another begins. They are a continuous visual strip, and although each house may vary in detail through individual choice or because they were built at different times, the overall effect is of one unit. Because transport was so expensive they could only be built from local materials. Colours were applied subtly in the manner of an artist. During the 17th century the idea of building a group of houses as if they were really one great house was introduced. The central and end houses were given more importance by being placed slightly forward (about 150 mm or 6 in) from the ones

between and often had slightly different windows and roofs with pediments like a classical temple. This idea of grouping houses was expanded in the 18th century into grand squares and circuses for the largest houses, with gradually diminishing houses in the streets behind. The whole plan was worked out with mathematical precision, using classical formulae for finding proportions pleasing to the eye. Each individual house and each detail of it followed the same precise system. Outwardly similar, each house was built to individual taste within. The largest and most splendid houses were called First Rate; Second Rate were slightly smaller with simpler details, and so on down to the smallest Fifth Rate house. This was extremely simple, with a minimum of ornament, nevertheless it still

exactly followed the classical proportions used for the largest houses. These terraces used very few contrasting materials, they were either all stone, all stucco, all brick (sometimes with stucco additions) or all weather-boarded timber. The effect was simple, often grand, dull occasionally. During the 19th-century terraces continued to be designed in this way, but with the growing number of single suburban dwellings based on the rambling designs of buildings in the country, there was a return to the medieval concept of individual design. There was one important difference: whereas the medieval builder had limited materials, the 19th- and 20th-century builders have had a country-wide selection to choose from. The effect was far from simple, never grand, always lively and interesting.

15

1

2

THE HOUSES ILLUSTRATED **on this and the next six pages show something of the great variety of landscape background that occurs in Britain and how they fit against it.**

1 This placid river quietly slipping between flat water meadows is the Kennet at Kintbury in Berkshire. The simple Victorian cottage is built of red brick made from clay dug nearby. The red is complementary to the surrounding greens and about the same chroma and value.

2 Behind this traditional whitewashed cottage in south-west Ireland is the Burren, a great grey limestone desert. The thatched roof is just a warmer shade of grey. In front is the Atlantic. The cottage walls and those surrounding the fields are made from the same grey limestone, but those of the cottage are painted sparkling white.

3 Another study in grey and white, this time on the west coast of Scotland: if the house had been left in its local grey stone colour, it would have been visually lost, instead of providing a visual focus.

4 The lush greens of south Devon parkland with steeply folded little hills, full of variety and interest, contrast with the square precision of this late 17th-century manor built of red brick not much different in colour from the red earth all round.

5 A mountain landscape in Scotland; the huge mass of rock would completely dominate the houses if they were not picked out in white.

6 The seasons change the colours of the landscape, but not as much as the farmer. This farmhouse in Suffolk has a traditional pink finish which blends well with yellow corn or ploughed earth because it has similar chroma.

7 A fertile valley in central Scotland surrounded by high moorland. The grey stone walls around the fields together with the grey houses form a counterpoint against the rich green. Here the landscape dominates.

8 This small cottage was once the focal point in an undulating Tyneside landscape; now it is dwarfed by the power station which makes it seem quite out of place. A bright colour, such as a high chroma red, would be one way to redress the balance.

3

4

5

7

6

8

1

2

3

4

1   The trees in this valley in Cumbria were carefully planted as in a park; the houses are incidental, built of local stone and solid as the hills. Left in their natural colour or simply whitewashed, the houses, like the roads, complete a landscape whose main elements are the superb swinging lines of the hills and the tall deciduous trees.

2   The dominating feature of this flat landscape in Galway is the field walls built of huge rocks, hardly suitable for house building. The cottages are either mud or built of a finer, smaller stone from neighbouring areas. They are always colour-washed, some in shades of buff, blue grey, pink or orange but most are traditional white.

3   A farm in a flat valley in Cumbria with its outbuildings and yard walls seen against the trees planted to protect it from the prevailing wind. The outlines of the buildings in pale natural stone are distinctly framed against this background, whereas they would have been lost in an open landscape.

4   These cottages on flat land in Bedfordshire are more thatched roof than wall; if it were not for the colour-washed walls with their rounded gable windows, they would merge with the background almost completely.

5   An upland landscape in Devon, crowded with detail; complicated field shapes and crops, a great variety of trees both in type and size, the land folded and worn into intricate shapes. There is no grand design here, it is like the setting for a model railway. The houses, sensibly positioned for convenience and climate, are on sites probably used for thousands of years.

6   A flat, treeless landscape in Caithness in the north of Scotland edged by the sea just over the horizon and by distant mountains. The low normally insignificant crofts form major points of interest. Their stone or thatched roofs blend with the landscape; only their low, straight, whitewashed walls and their silhouettes against the sky make them stand out.

7   This tower-house farm, typical of many in the Border areas fortified against marauders, was sited for defence and commands the whole of this Cumbrian valley. The stone walls spread away from it like the legs of a spider.

5

6

7

19

1

2

3

20

1 A Gloucestershire stone village in the Cotswolds: Stanway, full of limestone cottages dating back to the 16th century. The roof tiles as well as the walls are all made from the same type of stone.

2 A Kent village: Tenterden, built on the edge of the Weald where there is little good building stone. Most of the houses have timber frames covered in a variety of cladding: weatherboards, clay tiles or wood panels imitating stone. They are far from being alike but they look well together because of the similarity of scale and proportion and a generous use of white: they have the same window proportions and the same direct simplicity of feeling.

3 A narrow passageway in Marlborough, Wiltshire. It makes a spy-hole in an otherwise straight row of houses to a brightly coloured cottage garden behind.

4 Lismore, Co. Waterford, a typical painted town in southern Eire, the colours running through the town like a continuous mural.

5 Houses round the harbour at Aberaeron in Dyfed on the west coast of Wales. This is a Regency New Town attributed to John Nash. The houses are plastered, carefully related in design and colour, providing an excellent lesson in simple town-planning.

6 Bedford Square, London, built 1775-80, possibly designed by Thomas Leverton, in the grand manner of the times. Although each house is huge by present-day standards, they are only part of the splendid concept of a brick and stucco square built round a garden with trees.

7 Late 18th-century terrace in Bath, Avon. Only two colours are in evidence: yellow limestone with green grass and trees, a simplicity that gives the town its marvellous feeling of cohesion.

8 16th- and 17th-century houses in Culross on the Firth of Forth, Scotland, carefully restored by the National Trust for Scotland to their original colours. Warm and inviting they demonstrate how colour can transform a cold, grey town.

9 A painted stucco terrace in Brighton, East Sussex, imitating the uniform quality of stone used in other areas.

4

5

6

7

8

9

21

1

2

22

1 A distinguished stucco house in London built about 1820 with every classical detail precisely carried out. Originally the plaster rendering would have been colour-washed to simulate stone. Now, like most houses of this period, it has been solidly painted over.

2 A line of homely semi-detached houses built about 1905 in a north London suburb. Although bearing a superficial similarity, each one has its individual characteristics, forming a rich variety of shapes. Many different materials are employed: half-timbering, plastering, brickwork, tile-hanging, timber-framed and leaded light windows.

3 A group of 17th-century town houses near the cathedral at Ripon in North Yorkshire. The subdued colours of the plasterwork, enlivened by picking out the windows and doors in white, form a pleasant harmony with the natural magnesian limestone.

4 Sedate neo-Georgian detached houses at Welwyn Garden City built about 1925; similar designs are still being built today. The design is restrained; a red clay pantile roof with similarly-coloured brick walls. Picked out in white, the door and window proportions appear solid and humourless.

5 Three-storey terrace town houses built in north London in 1968. The general design follows the current international style: plenty of glass arranged in horizontal bands, subdued overall colour brightened by patches of primary colours, all designed with straight hard lines.

6 A road on a housing development built during the 1960s; just a row of houses. Little attempt has been made by the planning authority or the developers to create unity, but the design, unlike 5, has a rustic, homely quality although using similar materials.

7 A typical street of late 19th century artisan houses in West Hampstead, London, carefully designed with traditional craftsmanship in mind. Originally the twin front gardens were full of shrubs, now replaced by dustbins. New trees have been planted in the pavement to restore the visual balance.

8 Terrace houses in Crawley, Sussex built in 1968 and designed by Fitzroy Robinson. The asbestos cladding is a substitute for blue slate.

3

4

5

SPINNEY CLOSE

6

7

8

Colour history

PAINT HAS BEEN USED from earliest times to identify the outside of houses so that they were signalled out in an untamed landscape as places of refuge, or protection. White was used almost universally, since it showed up well and was easy to make from chalk dust with size and milk used as binders. As a colour it still represents 50% of all exterior paint sales. However simple homes had only their front walls painted white, or even just the door surround. Farms consisting of one long building containing both people and cattle had the part for human occupation painted to avoid confusion. Castles were usually painted white, hence the White Tower of the Tower of London, whose original paint has long since washed off.

Most ancient building materials are now considered rare and beautiful. Few were especially valued in the past.

The disadvantage of painting all houses white in a town or village was that they lost their identities; the result was that a stone castle, supposed to be strong, merely looked like a larger version of the easily destroyed timber buildings near by. Colours were introduced to solve this problem and the outlines of the stonework were painted in. The first colours came from the artists and weavers who decorated the inside, the next step was to use colours outside as pure decoration. The original stone designs were developed with floral embellishments.

The earliest colours were ones which did not need elaborate processing. Bullocks' blood, also used for making mud floors dust-proof, was still being used in the latter half of the 19th century and the other colours, soot, charcoal and the earth colours, yellow ochre from Oxfordshire, umber from Cornwall and Devon red ochre, are still some of the best and most permanent pigments known today. As a group, these colours have a disadvantage since they are all dull red, brown or yellow. Weavers were able to use much brighter colours made from boiling plants with wool in water but this method was hardly suitable for house decoration. A second generation of cheap pigments was evolved by applying heat to various common substances to make burnt umber and burnt sienna. More complicated and expensive chemical processes gave the Middle Ages red, white and yellow from lead, green from copper, vermilion from sulphur and quicksilver, blue from cobalt, madder from the root of the madder plant, azure or ultramarine lapis lazuli (very expensive and hardly used for outside decoration), malachite green from copper resinate, gamboge, azurite, Naples yellow, orpiment and verdigris, from oxides of lead, antimony and tin.

The recipes for making colours were jealously guarded and as a result have in a few cases been lost; others, lethal if misused, have been replaced by more modern, safe pigments.

The medieval colour range was short of good bright yellows and blues cheap enough to use in quantity. Prussian blue when discovered became the most popular blue during the 18th century until a cheap method of making azure or ultramarine became available in 1800. During the 19th century the various colours based on chrome became available: chrome yellow and Brunswick green replacing orpiment and verdigris; the coaltar colours, such as alizarin, were much cheaper alternatives to traditional colours like madder. During the 20th century many new colours have been developed and the problem today is not one of limitation but of selection.

The development of colours was paralleled by a similar development in paint manufacture. All paints consist basically of a base material mixed with a binder. To this can be added a pigment for colour, a solvent to make the paint spread easily and a drier to make it dry quickly. Until the 20th century painters ground and mixed their own paints, changing the formula to suit different conditions. For instance, the south side of a house would be given more oil to stop the paint drying out too much in the sun, while the north side would have more body to protect it against frosts. Today paints are designed to be suitable for all conditions but some of the old formulations have proved to last an astonishingly long time, especially where they are not exposed to the sun.

There are several types of painting used for decoration outside. The earliest and simplest is lime wash tempera distemper. A typical recipe of 1356 calls for two parts of chalk dust to one of size made from boiled strips of leather. At various times egg yolk, milk, beer, wine, salt and potatoes were added and plaster of Paris used instead of, or with, lime. A recipe of 1820 suggests one pound of potatoes to two pounds of lime white to one gallon of water (Stuart). A recipe of 1875 (Davidson) is for half a bushel of lime, one pound of common salt, half a pound of sulphate of zinc and one gallon of milk. Recent recipes are much simpler again, some of the old recipes sounding more like a good meal than a good paint. A good lime wash can be made up by steeping a hundredweight of dry quicklime in one gallon of raw linseed oil for sixteen hours and then thinning with water to a creamy consistency, before applying two coats. Since none of these paints will last more than a year or two before another coat is necessary, medieval painters did not worry too much about the permanence of their colouring agents, which could be severely affected by the lime and mixing. All the earth colours, however, were generally quite safe. Wide overhanging eaves were used to protect the lime wash; gutters and downpipes had the same purpose originally, but constant repainting in time builds up a thick protective coat of lime.

Although oil paint was known in the 13th century, it was very expensive and it was not until the beginning of the 18th century that it became extensively used for woodwork. The reason for this was that until then oak had been the chief timber and the only protection it needed was a little charring where it was in contact with the earth. With the introduction of deal – a much cheaper wood, when the great oak forests had been felled – paint had for the first time to take on a new role: that of protection. This introduced a complication since a paint which lasted a long time demonstrated colours which faded or interacted with each other when mixed. During the 18th century important houses had gilded window frames (which were probably of mahogany) but most houses were finished with a simple white lead paint. At the beginning of the 18th century the front doors were still oak and these were treated with a mixture of oil and varnish, a method used throughout the medieval period to protect timber against unnecessary marking. Later in the 18th century, when pine doors came into use, oil paint was used, protected by a coat of oil copal or similar varnish, a practice still followed today for first-class work. Colours popular at the end of the 18th century were grey, lead, ash, stone, buff, sage green, pea green, sea green, light willow green, grass green, apricot, peach, orange, fine yellow, fawn, olive green, light timber and brick. The increasing use of coal during the early 19th century polluted the atmosphere so much that it was impractical to use white outside. At first it was tinted with ochre or black, and later, towards the middle of the century, windows were painted a practical chocolate brown and front doors a dark Brunswick green, blue or black.

Stucco roman cement, invented by Parker

and popularised by John Nash, was originally either integrally coloured or lime washed to imitate stone (Bath stone was then fashionable in London), but the increasingly dirty atmosphere led to a change to oil paint, cream being chosen as nearest to the colour of Bath. As in fresco painting (an ancient technique of applying paint to internal plaster while it is still wet so that the colour and plaster become homogeneous), there was little point in mixing colour with the weak lime plasters of the Middle Ages – it was much simpler to give them a coat of colour-wash. When the much stronger stucco cements were invented around 1800 colour was introduced to match them to stone until the polluted atmosphere left them so dirty that oil paint was substituted. In the last forty years, coloured cements have been re-introduced in a range of earth colours for rendering and mortars. Cement-based paints have been used since 1830, when they were first introduced by Parker for painting timber to prevent dry rot. They have gradually replaced lime washes, since they last much longer, and the more sophisticated versions are used as alternatives to oil paint for walls.

Fine textured resin-based masonry paints, unlike cement paints, can be made in strong bright colours and are now used widely for first-class work.

Three houses painted in reproduction 18th-century colours.

1   House in Debenham, East Suffolk, painted in Orpiment.

2   Farm, at Hadleigh, West Suffolk, painted in Pale Vermilion.

3   House at Walsham-le-Willows in West Suffolk, painted in Minium.

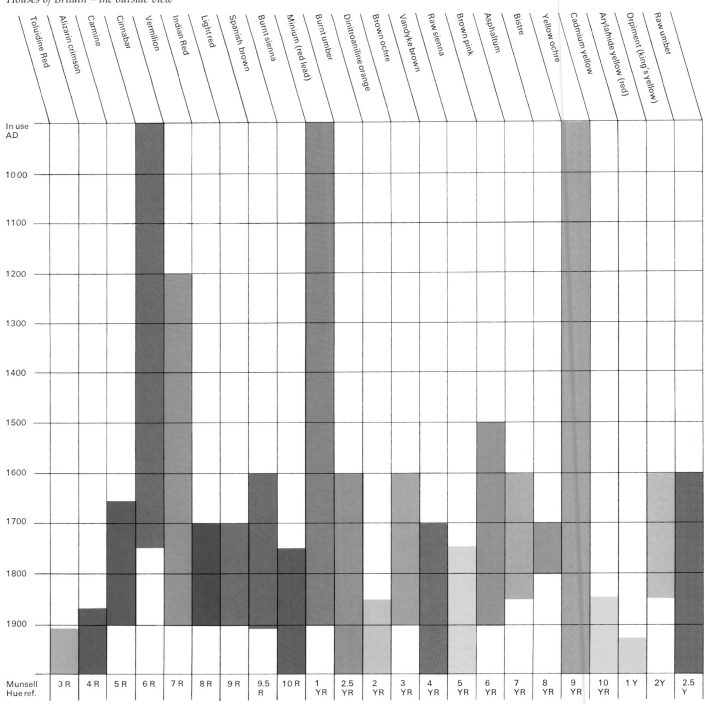

Toluidine Red | Alizarin crimson | Carmine | Cinnabar | Vermilion | Indian Red | Light red | Spanish brown | Burnt sienna | Minium (red lead) | Burnt umber | Dinitroaniline orange | Brown ochre | Vandyke brown | Raw sienna | Brown pink | Asphaltum | Bistre | Yellow ochre | Cadmium yellow | Arylamide yellow (red) | Orpiment (king's yellow) | Raw umber

In use AD
1000
1100
1200
1300
1400
1500
1600
1700
1800
1900

| Munsell Hue ref. | 3 R | 4 R | 5 R | 6 R | 7 R | 8 R | 9 R | 9.5 R | 10 R | 1 YR | 2.5 YR | 2 YR | 3 YR | 4 YR | 5 YR | 6 YR | 7 YR | 8 YR | 9 YR | 10 YR | 1 Y | 2Y | 2.5 Y |

R = red   YR = yellow red   Y = yellow   YG = yellow green   G = green   BG = blue green   B = blue   PB = purple blue   RP = red purple

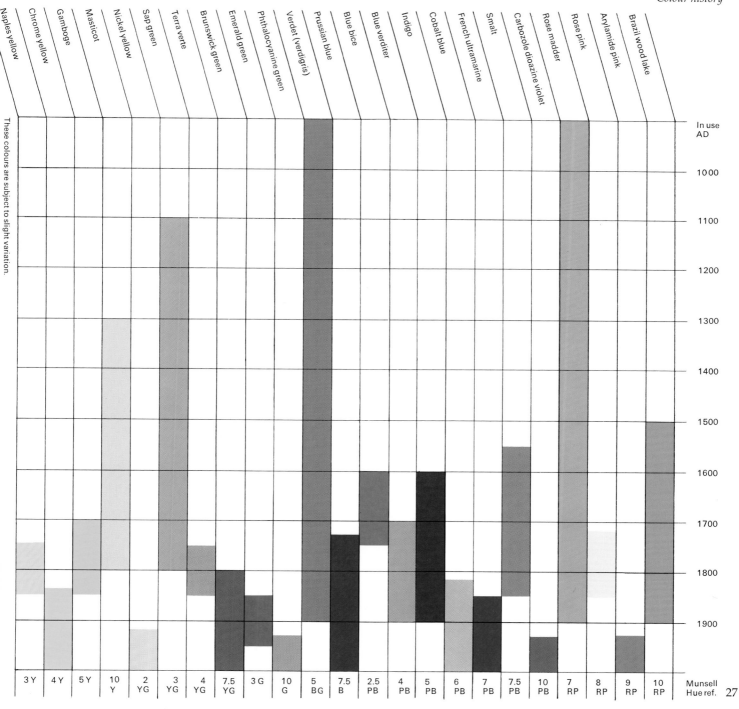

These colours are subject to slight variation.

| | Naples yellow | Chrome yellow | Gamboge | Masticot | Nickel yellow | Sap green | Terra verte | Brunswick green | Emerald green | Phthalocyanine green | Verdet (verdigris) | Prussian blue | Blue bice | Blue verditer | Indigo | Cobalt blue | French ultramarine | Smalt | Carbozole dioazine violet | Rose madder | Rose pink | Arylamide pink | Brazil wood lake | In use AD |

| 3 Y | 4 Y | 5 Y | 10 Y | 2 YG | 3 YG | 4 YG | 7.5 YG | 3 G | 10 G | 5 BG | 7.5 B | 2.5 PB | 4 PB | 5 PB | 6 PB | 7 PB | 7.5 PB | 10 PB | 7 RP | 8 RP | 9 RP | 10 RP | Munsell Hue ref. 27 |

R = red   YR = yellow red   Y = yellow   YG = yellow green   G = green   BG = blue green   B = blue   PB = purple blue   RP = red purple

Colours for houses

PAINTING A HOUSE is like taking part in a huge communal picture in which the rest of the painting is done either by nature or by other people. The picture is not static, it changes as we move about, with the time of day, with the seasons, with new planting, new buildings and with alterations to old ones. Any house is just a fragment of this picture, nevertheless it has the power to make or mar the overall scene. In the past people used their creative talents in painting their homes with great imagination in varied but always subtly blending colours. The last vestiges of this great tradition can still be seen in the towns of the extreme west of Ireland. It has never been recognised as an art form, partly because of the physical difficulty of hanging a street in a gallery and partly because it is always changing, as paint fades and is renewed. Also it is a communal art which cannot be pigeon-holed to any one person. Fortunately many great artists of the past found inspiration in ordinary street scenes and recorded them in paint.

Today, although town planning legislation has taken away the individual's ultimate responsibility and enjoyment of free design, it is still possible to derive pleasure from the careful choice and application of colour to a house. Only in the case of a house listed by the local authority as having historic or particular architectural interest is there likely to be any control and then only a sensible restriction if the proposed decoration is out of keeping.

Following the principles of decoration that were so successful in the past, first take a long look at the house and its surroundings.

The first limitation is the colour and intensity of the daylight in Britain. Colours that look perfectly in keeping with the sunny, clear skies of the Mediterranean would look too harsh in the greyer light of the north. Since bright light is uncomfortable for the eyes, colours must be strong in order to be seen clearly. Viewed in a dimmer light they appear too bright. It is easy to see this if you look at a brick house while the sun is alternately shining and then going behind a cloud. The brickwork colours look much more intense when the sun is hidden.

The second limitation is the colours of the surroundings: the colours which go best with Cotswold stone and a rolling green countryside will be different from those that look best by the sea or in a red-brick/blue slate industrial town. In every area there are always colours that at once look in keeping.

In many areas there are distinctive traditions in the use of colour that may be a useful rule. The eastern counties of England and Scotland, particularly those with a local tradition of rendering or plastering, use colours applied solidly over the wall. Usually only the window frames and doors are picked out in another colour, often white or pale grey. Typical wall colours are the pink associated with Suffolk and pale buffs and yellows of Fife. Much stronger colours such as deep earth red, orange, blue and green are also common. The weather-boarded houses of Essex and Hertfordshire are traditionally painted black – originally tarred like ships – with windows and doors outlined in white. In Kent weather-boarded houses are usually white. In stone areas of Yorkshire and farther north, colour is rarer: the houses are usually left in their natural colour, though many are painted white as they probably all were once.

In the western counties of England, Wales and Scotland, the strongest traditions are black-and-white, especially in the upland areas. In central Wales, Cumbria and the west coast of Scotland, there are many cottages and farms painted white with the corner stones (quoins), windows and doors painted black. They look very effective against a mountainous landscape. In Cheshire there is a more recent tradition of black-and-white half-timbered houses that has spread throughout the country. In lowland areas, the use of colour is much more adventurous, nowhere more so than in the far west of Ireland.

The easiest way to choose colours for a particular house is to take a photograph of it straight on and enlarge it on a photocopier to A4. The outline can then easily be traced off, using thin white or tracing paper, and a number of colour schemes tried out with a range of felt pens. Start with a selection that seems most satisfying and best fits the surroundings. Experiment as much as possible, then take the best drawings outside and compare the house with them. The ultimate scheme is the one that you instinctively respond to: it is not the one you know is right, it is the one you feel is right. In a dirty atmosphere use areas of light colour on window surrounds and other features, contrasted against a darker general colour on the main walling. The house will then look cleaner longer due to this contrast. Small areas of white are always useful giving sparkle in conjunction with a darker colour.

Contrasting colours on carefully restored houses in King's Lynn, Norfolk.

1

2

3

4

5

6

7

8

9

10

1 Painted stucco rendering simulating stonework on an early 19th-century house at Aberaeron, Dyfed, Wales.

2 Painted corner-stones against a rough-cast wall on a house at Cahir, Co. Tipperary, Eire.

3 Whitewashed rubble stonework outlining the smoothly-finished sandstone corner-stones. A barn in Cumbria.

4 Pink wash carefully mixed by the owner of a cottage in Clarecastle, Co. Clare, Eire.

5 The scarlet window frame on a cottage otherwise entirely painted in the same cream. Galway, Eire.

6 Early l9th-century house in Ennis, Co. Clare, Eire, with selected mouldings picked out in black. The selection completely distorts the architectural design of the house but makes it sparkle.

7 Black and white used to reinforce the architectural design of this late 18th century cottage in Cumbria.

8 Related pink and purple-brown on a cottage in Wiltshire.

9 A restrained colour scheme on a 19th-century cottage at Kintbury in Berkshire.

10 Early l9th-century house partially converted to a shop. Aberaeron, Dyfed, Wales.

11 A typical farm entrance in Cumbria, built about the middle of the 18th century.

12 A subtly decorated doorway in Oban, Argyll, in Scotland.

13 Two front doors on a low-cost housing scheme in north London built in 1970. One is coloured brown, for dustbins, the other coloured red, for people.

14 Early 18th-century door in a rectory in Wiltshire. The limestone surround has been painted as well as the door, destroying the original character.

15 A late 18th-century door in Clarecastle, Co. Clare.

16 Traditional graining on the door of an 18th-century manor house in Cumbria.

17 Traditional graining on an 18th-century door in Cashel, Co. Tipperary, Eire.

18 1930s door in Co. Clare, Eire.

19 Early l9th-century Gothic Revival door in Derbyshire.

11

12

13

14

15

16

17

18

19

1 Early 19th-century house in Perth, Scotland. The colours are well chosen but curiously only the columns have been picked out in white. In stucco houses of this period the correct treatment is either to paint the house in one colour, since stucco is trying to simulate stone, or alternatively paint all projections from the main wall face a light colour leaving the base colour on the wall only. This avoids any distortion of the design, so the full architectural effect can be appreciated – very important in a design as carefully worked out as this.

2 Early 19th-century Gothic Revival cottage in Wiltshire with a colour scheme carefully worked out to emphasise its architectural features.

3 Late 18th-century house in Lincolnshire. It has become a rule to paint the entire window frame white, the sill left in natural stone or painted a stone colour and only the front door in a colour, with downpipes and gutters in dark grey. The rules have been very effectively broken in this example.

4 Typical early 19th-century stone terraced cottages in Carlisle, Cumbria. The different owners have chosen colours that blend well together and set off the colour of the sandstone. Note the small attic windows practically at floor level to avoid the cost and complication of building dormer windows.

5 Late 18th-century farmhouse in Cumbria. The pale blue and white paint is effectively set off by the dull textured rendering. Probably applied during the last century over the original stonework.

6 16th-century merchants' houses much altered in later centuries but restored to their original colour. King's Lynn, Norfolk.

7 Delicately coloured early 19th-century farmhouse in Cumbria.

8 17th-century town house in Thaxted, Essex. This is a timber-frame house, plastered and painted in a deep, traditional pink. White is used to emphasise the architectural features and the dark brown door looks effective against the pink. The base is painted with black tar, another traditional treatment.

32

1

2

3

4

5

6

7

8

1

2

1, 2 This mid-19th-century terrace in Mortlake, Greater London, is typical of many built at this time throughout the country. The Welsh slate roof slopes at two different angles to give more room inside; called a mansard roof, after a French 17th-century architect who used it frequently. It was cheaper to put rooms in the roof with projecting windows than to build another storey. It also kept the houses lower visually, a device repeated with the basement which is half below ground. Only the important rooms on the ground and first floors are given visual emphasis. Classical design is largely concerned with order of precedence. In this case the relative importance of each floor is revealed by the size of the windows; the small bedrooms in the roof for children and servants are least important, next come the kitchen and scullery in the basement, then the main bedrooms on the first floor and lastly the drawing room and dining room on the ground floor. Horizontally, the centre pair of houses are made more important by being advanced slightly and by being given the medallion centred over the heavy cornice moulding below the roof. There are other subtle distinctions in the details, both outside and in, all designed to give an ordered appearance. Before making any alterations, it is important to understand the care with which a design such as this was carried out. The strength of the design is shown in these two quite different methods of decorating, though they are both sympathetic to the design. In **1**, the house appears much as it was intended, stone coloured walls with projecting mouldings picked out in white; only the different coloured doors give any hint of individuality. In **2**, each house has been painted in related colours; the individual ownership is clearly defined but the terrace still appears as a unit.

3

4

3, 4, 5 Three ways of painting a row of early 19th-century farm cottages in Sussex. There is no order of precedence here, but the proportions are so carefully worked out that, provided the row is kept as a whole, a great variety of colour schemes would be equally successful.

5

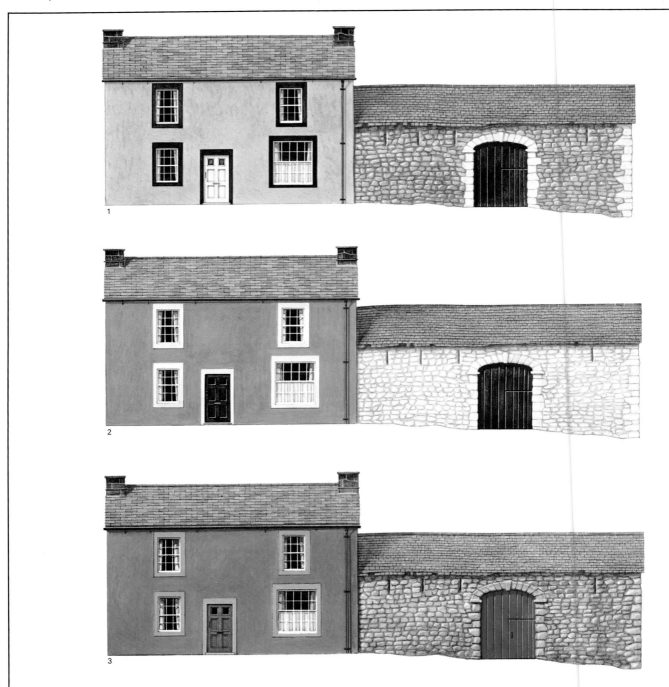

1, 2, 3 This farmhouse in Cumbria is typical of thousands of such houses in the stony upland regions of Britain. Built in the 17th century, it was the latest development of a design that goes back at least three thousand years, to a time when animals and people lived under one roof, divided by a light partition. In remote parts of the country houses were still being built like this in the 19th century. Like this house they were always built on a slope, with the animals at the bottom end so that the urine could drain away without inconvenience. To differentiate between the two uses of the building, the section for people was painted (as in this case), and the part for animals left unpainted. Three different ways of painting the farm are shown, each with colours commonly used in the 18th century. There is no need to add the porches and coach lamps so often applied today; they are like putting a feather hat on a weather-beaten farmer. Good colour is all that is needed.

4, 5 Neither of these versions of an early 17th-century timber-frame town house in Suffolk is original, but they show how the design was altered in a recent 'restoration'. The hallmark of vernacular building is its consistency. In this case the house would have been plastered over, like the majority of other houses in the area, to keep out draughts and wet. Both the lower windows would have had shutters and all would have the same diagonal lead glazing. The original door would have been much lower with plain boards. The restoration, instead of sympathetically putting back what was there, has invented a quite new facade: a fake of a fake.

6, 7 Two versions of an 18th-century town house in Torryburn, Dunfermline, in Scotland. The stone walls are plastered in harling (pronounced 'hurling'), a traditional Scottish finish consisting of 1:2:8 cement/lime/pebbles and sharp sand, thrown onto the wall and then colour-washed. The roof is covered with pantiles and one gable end is made from squared stones, called 'crowstepping'. This design feature was originally developed to save cutting extremely hard local stone and is widely used in Scotland and Ireland.

8, 9 This house in Ballyvaughan, Co. Clare, Eire, built about 1910, could have been soberly coloured as **8**. Instead, it has been painted as **9**, showing the adaptability of a regular classic design.

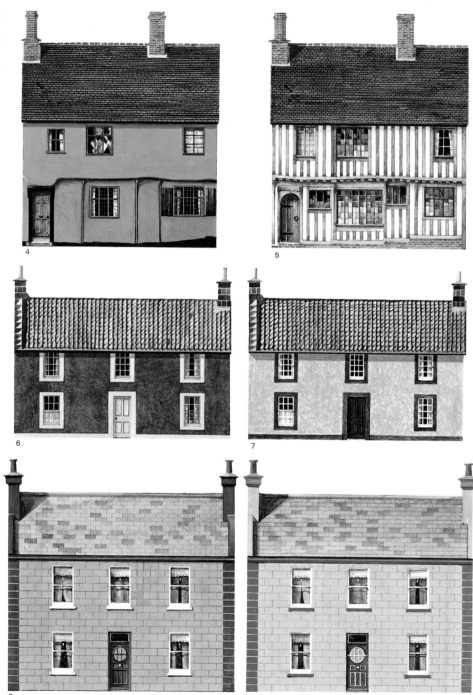

4

5

6

7

8

9

37

1, 2, and **3** show three designs of semi-detached houses built in the first half of the 20th century. Many of these houses are now in need of renovation, particularly in the case of those which were originally finished in pebble-dash. Because these houses have such a variety of shapes, great care must be taken in working out their colour schemes. Unlike the classical Georgian house whose simple design will accept strong colours, if appropriate, these designs are best carried out in similarly-toned colours so that one feature is not emphasised more than others.

1 A pair of semi-detached cottages designed by Henry Cayley and exhibited at the Cheap Cottages Exhibition of 1905 held at Letchworth Garden City, Hertfordshire,

under the patronage of a number of people, including the then Archbishop of Canterbury, Ebenezer Howard, Edwin Lutyens, Rudyard Kipling, Asquith and Balfour. The full list demonstrates the wide interest taken by the public at this time in low-cost house design. The upper version shows the houses painted light cream, with the bay windows picked out in Mid Stone with white front doors. The lower scheme is in light green picked out with white bays and blue front doors. The first scheme is warm, the second, cool in feeling.

2 Two ways of painting a pair of semi-detached houses originally designed by Patrick Abercrombie about 1912; at Molesworth, near Chester. The upper house

has been painted in Mid Stone with green shutters and white front doors. This is a conservative colour scheme adopted traditionally for cottages. The second scheme is in pink, set off by the pale grey shutters and window frames. The first version makes the houses look distinguished, a suitable colour scheme for an estate. The second makes them look much prettier; more suitable for the open countryside.

3 A pair of speculative semi-detached houses designed by Welch, Cachmaille-Day and Lander and built in 1938 as part of an estate in Edgware, London. The roofs are covered with green-glazed pantiles that were so fashionable at this period. This was a durable and practical finish, a version of the

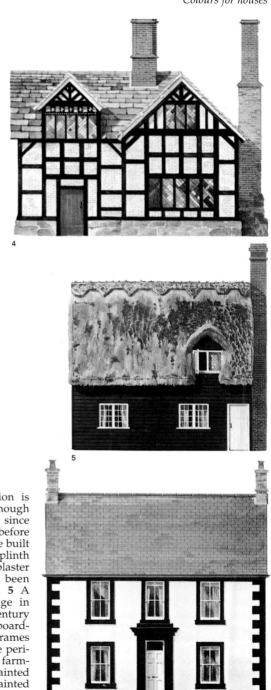

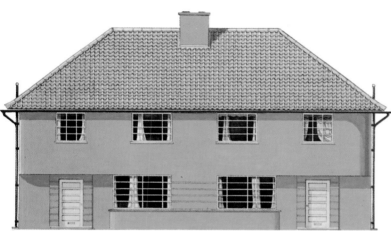

3

traditional black-glazed pantiles of East Anglia. Compared with the previous two designs which are vertical in character these have sleek, horizontal proportions. The earlier designs still belong to the era of horsedrawn transport. These houses belong to the new period of the fast car. The metal windows have long horizontal proportions, like the doors. In addition further horizontal accent is given by the grooved rendering. Originally the houses would have been in white, probably picked out in dark green. Two alternatives are shown, the upper one in beige with dark blue window bars and white doors, the lower example in golden brown with yellow doors and windows. The overall factor in both these schemes is the roof.

4, 5, 6 The black-and-white tradition is strong throughout the British Isles, although not older than the mid 18th century, since black outside paint was not available before then. **4** is a typical Cheshire farmhouse built in the early 17th century. The roof and plinth are sandstone, the original lath and plaster infill between the timbering has been replaced with brick painted white. **5** A weather-boarded timber-frame cottage in Hertfordshire, built in the late 18th century with a straw thatch roof. The weatherboarding is tarred black with the window frames in white in the manner of ships of the period. **6** is an early 19th-century stone farmhouse in Cumbria plastered and painted white with projecting mouldings painted black.

39

Design influences

LOGICALLY, all houses in Britain should look the same. The pressures for conformity have nearly always been stronger than the desire for individuality. In medieval times it was the King, the Church, the Municipality or the Guilds that made sure everyone did the same thing (Henry II had the whole of London painted white to be like Paris). Today we have very detailed building bye laws and planning acts to keep our houses in order. However, uniformity is not only convenient for administration, it has always been easier for the individual.

Until the invention of the blue-print in 1842 and the development of modern drafting techniques, drawings could not be copied except laboriously by hand and it was difficult to convey detailed instructions. If there were any drawings they were very simple and related only to the overall design and proportions of the house. Old contracts, in the absence of drawings, could only refer to copying another building at a convenient distance, perhaps with certain improvements. Later builders used pattern books of designs, such as those of Palladio or Batty Langley, widely published between 1650 and 1850. This was a very good discipline, since everything had to be done by eye on site (even the pattern books had to be interpreted to fit the individual job) and every visual factor, such as the curve of a hill, the position of the church tower or the building next door, could all be taken easily into account. The craftsmen had to work like sculptors, but to a general pattern, and this was all that was needed to create the subtle variations on a theme which constitute the charm of an old village or town. It needed a little creative talent to achieve, but nothing rare or superhuman. The blue-print allowed a clear break with this tradition by making it possible to send out detailed drawings to a number of different builders for competitive tendering. This led to the modern building contract with its references to legally binding detailed drawings and specifications made with the designer's eye on his office wall, not on the site itself. Released from the practical need to copy a local building, designers found they were free to measure up and reproduce anything they found on their travels or any fantasy they could think up. Although developers kept to repetitive designs (since it was cheaper) the private client expected his architect to invest his designs with all the knowledge that travel could bring and to choose his materials from amongst the huge variety that the railway and canal systems had made available. The 19th century saw the first breakthrough for the individual in building history and the firm establishment of the architectural profession to serve him. The only control was fashion.

Reaction was swift: by the end of the 19th century many thoughtful people were advocating a return to the homely designs of the 16th and 17th centuries and an 'honest' use of traditional building materials. This turned out to be just another dream, since it was impossible to re-create the ancient system of building using drawings and modern contracts. The old system did not fit an industrialised, fast-moving society. Gradually, therefore, a new way of designing has evolved, quick to draw, specify, cost and build, which suits factory-made building materials and which can be assembled with cheap, largely unskilled labour. Because it has eliminated the skilled creative craftsman on site and concentrated all design decisions on a drawing board in an office, only the most talented architects have been able to produce great buildings. Reaction to the excesses of the 19th century resulted fifty years later in planning legislation which has successfully curbed individuality by making all designs subject to the decision of lay committees. The same legislation has ensured that most houses are built either by local authorities or by developers, thus further reinforcing conformity.

The map on the opposite page shows the main influences on the design of vernacular buildings in Britain. It is not intended to show in detail all the local variations on a map of this size. In particular the geology of Britain, which is as complicated as any in the world, can vary greatly in the space of a square mile. It is possible to get a wall built of granite, limestone or sandstone, under a slate roof with brick window surrounds; all local materials in parts of Cumbria. Any long journey through Britain will demonstrate the broad regional variations of building material shown on the map. Timber is not shown since it was once universally used and many houses from the 16th century onwards used imported timber when indigenous timber was no longer available. The ethnic divisions are broadly shown. Although people today change their houses fairly frequently this is quite a new development; before the 19th century the population was more static.

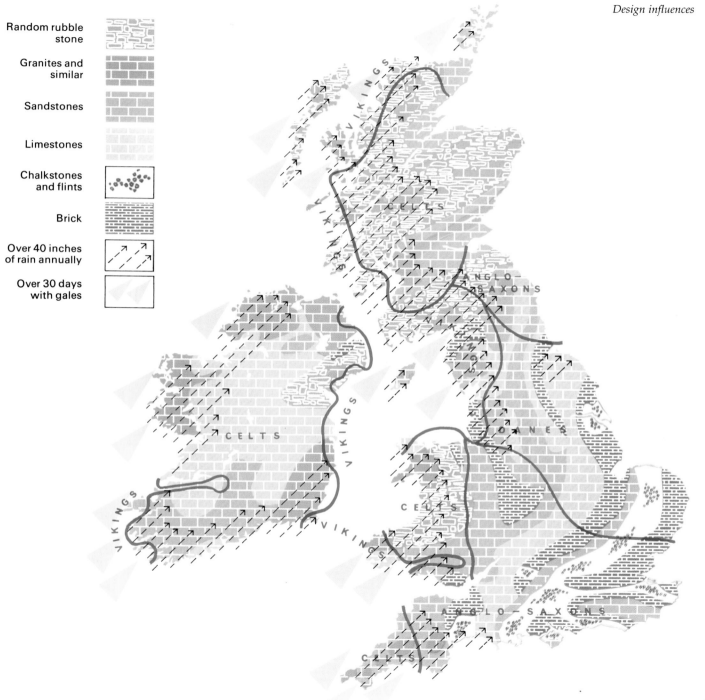

Random rubble stone

Granites and similar

Sandstones

Limestones

Chalkstones and flints

Brick

Over 40 inches of rain annually

Over 30 days with gales

VIKINGS
CELTS
ANGLO-SAXONS
DANES

Building in timber

THE NATURAL APPEARANCE of Britain would be a series of islands almost entirely covered with dense forest, if it had not been for the introduction of agriculture five thousand years ago and the subsequent demands for shipbuilding, industry (pottery, iron and charcoal) and the need to gather fuel and build houses. From about thirty million hectares of forest at that time, we now have only two and three-quarter million hectares, and of those only a few are primeval.

Until three hundred years ago timber was the universal building material throughout most of Britain. It was the cheapest, quickest, most adaptable and re-usable method of house construction. It was also the most flammable: which is why cities like London, once entirely built in timber, have been replaced with brick and stone, leaving a completely false idea of the importance of timber construction in history.

When the last Ice Age melted away ten thousand years ago, uncovering Scotland, northern England, most of Ireland and Wales (southern Britain was never entirely covered in ice), the first forests to grow were birch, poplar, rowan, willow and fir (Scots pine). These are still the commonest trees in Scotland. About eight thousand years ago oak, elm and hazel forests developed in the south as the country quickly warmed from a sub-Arctic climate to a Mediterranean peak six thousand years ago. At this time ash, alder and lime appeared for the first time followed four thousand years ago by beech and hornbeam in southern England. At this point natural introductions ceased; it was the Romans who brought the Spanish chestnut, walnut and fruit trees. Later, as the world was explored, the British gathered all the species they could grow from tropical palms to monkey puzzles.

The best timber was oak, which, suitably selected and cared for, gradually becomes as hard as stone with an indefinite life. Many old oak houses have been built from timbers of still older houses or ships. Although oak was and still is the commonest tree in southern Britain, it was more difficult to fell and harder to work than other timber. Oak was therefore reserved for important buildings and ordinary houses were built from willow, hornbeam, elm and chestnut. Since none of these timbers has the lasting qualities of oak, the houses built with the other timbers have rarely survived. This fact, together with the increasing wealth of Britain since the 16th century which enabled ordinary people to afford oak, has given the false impression that all timber houses were built of this wood.

Carpenters in the early Middle Ages were called wrights. They worked with axes with a skill now forgotten, smoothing the timber with adzes, and drilling holes with augers. They also had a number of different saws; but it was not until the 17th century that carpenters had anything like a modern tool kit. Seasoning was carried out by putting the timber in running streams to wash out the sap, but although this method was successful with woods like elm, English oak is impossible to season: cut an ancient piece, however hardened, and it will behave as if just taken from the tree. Oak after felling was stood up, so that inherent tendencies for movement could be studied, and was then used green.

The history of timber design reflects first the use of small, thin branches easily cut by early man, then the increasing use of large timbers as cutting and sawing methods improved and finally a return to smaller, weaker timbers when the great forests had been felled.

The first British homes were made of branches woven and strung together, often around a central pole or tree, and made waterproof with mud and turves, like giant baskets. The damp, leafy top soil was removed to a depth of a foot or so, a tradition which lasted well into the Middle Ages. This very ancient building method was still used in the 19th century in remote parts of Ireland, Scotland and Wales. In England it was used by charcoal burners in this century. Its descendant is the frame tent.

The improved felling methods developed in the Bronze Age made it possible to build more permanent houses out of solid logs, like those built in similar circumstances of plentiful timber by the early settlers in North America. The logs were laid either horizontally or vertically with the cracks between filled with mud. The only surviving example of this construction in Britain is the church at Greensted in Essex. These houses had vertical walls with a separately framed sloping roof – the classic design from which the architecture of ancient Greece and Rome and subsequently the Palladian style came.

As timber became scarce the frame house was developed, using far less timber. This no longer depended upon a monolithic construction but used separate posts and beams for the structure. ▶

A 19th-century timber home, Folkestone, Sussex.

1

2

3

4

Cruck houses: There has always been a close association between the builders of timber ships and houses. Cruck houses like ships upside down, were once widespread but are now rare. The best place to find them is in the Midlands, and particularly around Hereford. The simplest cruck frame consists of two carefully selected curving members, with their bases charred against rot, stuck into the ground with tops held together by a ridge piece like a keel. Cruck houses were the origin of the Gothic arch. Walls and roof had the same covering similar in principle to a Nissen hut.

In times when men and animals had to share the same building, the bay spacing of the crucks was critical. This was determined by the width needed for four oxen abreast. The disadvantage of sloping walls was that you could not stand upright at the edge of the building. To get over this problem a horizontal beam was inserted about halfway up, which could project beyond the crucks in such a way that a vertical wall could be formed below and a straight pitched roof above. This beam could also be used to brace the trusses together so that they did not depend on the holes in the earth for stability. In fact, the next step, having got a braced frame, was to take the crucks out of the earth altogether and stand them on dwarf walls where the ends would not rot. Its great merit was simplicity and some architects today have used the principle (now called the 'A' frame) for small houses in the country. In steel or concrete it is called a portal frame and is used for factories and agricultural buildings.

1   Cruck cottage at Didbrook, Gloucestershire.

2   15th-century close-spaced timber farmhouse in Tenterden, Kent.

3   16th-century gatehouse at Stokesay Castle, Shropshire.

4   Detail of the ornamental framing on 16th-century Little Morton Hall in Cheshire.

5   Late 18th-century Gothic Revival timbering at Plas Newydd, Llangollen, Clwyd.

6   Late 16th-century jettying at Lavenham, Suffolk.

7   Brick noggin replacing wattle and plaster on a house in Berkshire.

44

Square-frame houses, which originated from the classic log hut, can be roughly dated by the amount and size of timber they use. When timber was still fairly plentiful the vertical posts were close together, grooved for infilling panels, usually consisting of split oak laths wedged in and covered with a mixture of clay and straw and finally coated in lime plaster to fill up any cracks. As timber became scarcer the panels were enlarged and this meant that a secondary system of support was necessary for the mud infill. This consisted of short staves fitted into holes drilled in the main framework. Hazel branches were then woven between these like basketwork.

The result, when covered with clay, was known as wattle and daub. When the mud infill panels decayed they were frequently replaced in the 17th century and later by brick nogging which was more durable and fireproof, but which frequently led to the original construction rotting, since the bricks held water.

There are two broad structural classifications in square framing. In the first there is a series of main structural bays, as in the cruck frame, which means that the roof has to have extra horizontal supports transferring the weight of the rafters to these main frames; the other framing is just there to support the wall panels and first floor. In the second type (of no less antiquity) all the wall uprights share the load equally with the advantage that no large timbers are needed.

Ornament: The exposed timber-frame house was a natural opportunity for decoration. The simplest method was to pick out the panels in white or a colour, leaving the wood to weather a silver grey. Sometimes the wood was painted too, especially when the timbers were uneven, giving a more homogeneous effect. There is little difference between a narrow medieval town house and the stern of a galleon.

During the 15th century, a period with little church building, wood carvers turned their skill to houses and began to carve door and window frames, corner posts, the main horizontal beams at floor levels and the protective barge boards running up the ends of gabled roofs. They used flowing sinuous designs like the vine, symbols of the Church or the occupation of the owner. For a really splendid job the carving was picked out in bright colours and gilded. ▶

5

6

7

45

1

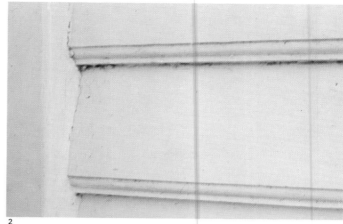

2

Cladding: There are four reasons for wanting to cover a timber frame. The first and earliest was that an overall covering was less likely to let in the weather, so early houses were covered in turves or rough planks. The second reason was to reduce the risk of fire, particularly in towns, by covering the frame with fireproof clay tiles, slates, brick or rendering, which has been used since the 13th century. The third, important reason was to protect the timber frame, which became necessary when imported softwoods were used in place of oak from the 18th century: 18th-century weather-boards usually have a moulding along the lower edge. Weather-boarding came back into vogue after the Second World War, but whereas it was always used horizontally in the past, it is now used vertically as well, following the Scandinavian style. The last reason was fashion. During the 18th century most people preferred the plain appearance of a stone or brick house.

1   Early 19th-century weather-boarded cottage in Sussex.

2   Detail of weather-boarding on 3.

3   Typical 18th-century weather-boarded terraced house in Mitcham.

4   18th-century plain tile hanging, Sussex.

5   Decorative tile hanging on a pair of cottages in Sussex built in 1902.

6   Slate hanging at Llanfrothen, Gwynedd, in North Wales.

7   Tile hanging on 1950s terraced houses in Teddington, Greater London.

3

4

5

6

7

1

2

3

4

5

6

48

7

8

9

10

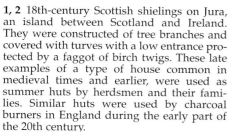

1, 2 18th-century Scottish shielings on Jura, an island between Scotland and Ireland. They were constructed of tree branches and covered with turves with a low entrance protected by a faggot of birch twigs. These late examples of a type of house common in medieval times and earlier, were used as summer huts by herdsmen and their families. Similar huts were used by charcoal burners in England during the early part of the 20th century.

3 14th-century curved-cruck long house used by peasant farmers in England, Wales and Scotland. Two-thirds of the house was used by the farmer and his family, the remainder for oxen and cows. The roof is thatched with reeds, the walls made from wattle, packed with mud and whitewashed.

4 Straight-cruck booth or cot used by herdsmen, a simple type of house introduced by the Saxons and Danes and still in use in the 15th century all over Britain. This example is based on Teapot Hall, now destroyed, near Horncastle, Lincolnshire. It exactly fitted a 19-ft (5.8m) cube. The roof was straw thatch on the upper part, slated near the ground.

5 14th-century curved-cruck cottage at Didbrook, Gloucestershire, shown restored to its original state. Note how small the door is by present-day standards.

6 Modern cruck house designed by Peter Boston near Hemingford Grey, Cambridgeshire, in 1960. The outside is entirely clad in Canadian western red cedar.

7 Box-frame farmhouse at Clifton-on-Teme, near Worcester, of a type widely built all over England during the 14th to 18th centuries.

8 Cottage in Harrow, Greater London, built in the early 1920s with cavity brick walls finished with plaster and applied half-timber. Designed by George Clare.

9 16th-century town house on the corner of Chancery Lane and Fleet Street, London, demolished in 1791. The timber work was elaborately carved like a galleon.

10 Timber-frame house plastered and pargetted – Framlingham, Suffolk. Built about 1680, the design is similar to contemporary work in Holland.

49

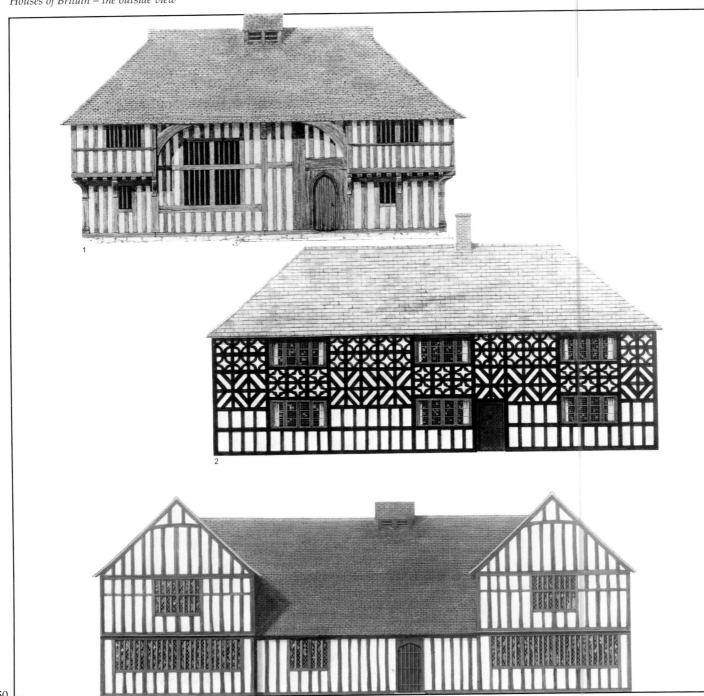

1

2

3

1 House of a yeoman (small freeholder) built at Egerton, Kent, about 1500 but typical of many built around the Weald in Kent, Surrey and East Sussex, and in Essex, Cambridgeshire and as far north as York. They were built during the 15th and 16th centuries. There is a high central hall with two-storey additions at the ends. Existing examples have later brick chimney stacks: this one is shown with its original smoke vent.

2 16th-century decorated timber-frame house: Morphany Hall, near Runcorn, Cheshire. About this time, carpenters began to decorate their rectangular framework with curved braces and numerous other members with no structural purpose. These were cut and shaped into diamond, lozenge and quatrefoil patterns and were particularly popular in the north-west of England. The Victorians loved them and painted the timbers black with white infills, following the nautical tradition of late 18th-century Bristol and Liverpool. The style thus developed became the prototype for the Tudor revival of the early 20th century.

3 14th-century 'H' plan house with a central hall aisled like a church: St Clere's Hall, St Osyth, Essex.

4 Victorian double cottage designed for a park, by Charles Richardson about 1860. He was a lecturer at the School of Design in Somerset House and wrote a number of books. Basically intended to be very cheap but with more expensive ornamental additions, such as the Tudor design shown.

5 Gardener's cottage in Forest Row, Sussex, designed by W. Henry White and built about 1900. The lower floor is cavity brickwork; the upper, solid 9-inch brick faced with half-timber treated with Stockholm tar, the spaces filled with plaster work.

6 A pair of cottages built at Sheepwash, Newtown, Hampshire, about 1920, designed by Francis Bacon. The lower walls are cavity brickwork, the upper have creosoted softwood frames with a single skin of brick between. The roof is straw thatch.

7 Semi-detached houses at Calne, Wiltshire, using local limestone and applied half-timbering. Built during the 1920s. The design is derived from the yeoman's house (**1**) and 'H' plan house (**3**).

4

5

6

7

1

2

3

4

1 Late 18th-century timber-frame town house at Ashburton on the southern side of Dartmoor in Devon. The ground floor is plastered, with grooves cut to simulate stonework; the upper floors are covered with small Cornish slates. The side walls are brick.

2 Late 18th-century timber-frame farmhouse near Rolvenden in Kent. The timber covering has been cut to simulate stone.

3 Early 19th-century timber-frame cottage near Henfield on the borders of East and West Sussex. The walls are plain tile hung and so is the roof. The outside shutters on the lower windows only were once a common feature on cottages in southern England. Larger houses had shutters inside.

4 Late 18th-century timber-frame town house at Hurstpierpoint, Sussex, covered with mathematical tiles simulating brickwork with timber corners simulating stone. The dormer windows in the roof have leaded lights, whereas the rest of the house has timber sashes. This was usual during the late 17th century and throughout the 18th.

5 17th-century timber-frame farmhouse near Smarden, Ashford, Kent. The ground floor is weather-boarded, the upper floor tile hung with fish-scale pattern tiles. These and similar patterns were often used in Kent, Surrey, Sussex and Hampshire during the 18th century. The windows have iron frames.

6 Late 18th-century timber-frame cottage in Streatham, London. This weather-boarded example is at the end of a terrace and is typical of the kind of house design once very common in the Surrey villages now buried in south London.

7 Early 19th-century pair of cottages at Fyfield, near Harlow, in Essex. The weather-boarding is tarred black, as is usual in Essex and Hertfordshire. The thatch is reed with a sedge capping. The chimney stack is turned at an angle above the roof line.

8 Timber-frame house built and designed by Bernard Le Mare in 1937 in Yorkshire. The weather-boarding is Canadian western red cedar. The general design with its flat bituminous felt roof, balcony and large windows is in the international style favoured by forward-looking architects of the day.

5

6 7

8

53

Building in mud

MUD SHARES WITH TIMBER the honour of being the oldest building material. It was used in earliest times to fill the crevices in the first timber houses. When the trees had been felled and timber became too expensive for simple buildings, mud in its various forms became a building material in its own right. It was used throughout the British Isles and the fact that so few mud houses are seen today is because it only lasts so long as it is well protected. A stone house can lose its roof and still be rebuilt a hundred years later; a mud house quickly becomes a mound of earth again.

To survive, mud houses must have good waterproof foundations, originally of timber or stone and later of brick. They must also have a roof with a good overhang, such as thatch, so that rain is thrown clear of the walls. Then they will last as long as they are cared for. It was a fortunate circumstance that mud and thatch were the two cheapest available building materials and were functionally suited to each other. What is more, since they are both weak materials, both the roof and walls had to be thick and this made the cottages they were used for far cooler in summer and far warmer in winter than other structural building materials available in the past. This well suited the pocket of the cottager. Another advantage of mud, though not of thatch, was that it did not require any great degree of skill in building, it was something the cottager could do for himself, perhaps with the aid of some friends, unlike carpentry, bricklaying or masonry.

There are four main methods of mud walling. They have different names depending on which part of the country they are being used in and their use depends on the kinds of earth locally available and on the technology of the area. The most primitive method, which was used in areas where there was thick turf, was simply to cut out close-cropped sods and lay them in broken courses like brickwork. These were once usual in all parts of Britain for the poorest homes as well as for animal shelters, but they were inherently temporary and few survive today. The commonest system is wet mud, called cob in Devon. Made from a nearby loamy earth, chosen because it will set well, mixed with a little chopped straw or reed to act as reinforcement, chalk if available to make it stronger, plus gravel, small stones and sand as ballast, all mixed together in a gluelike consistency. The mixture is then laid in layers from 6 to 12 in. (150 to 300 mm) thick depending on the locality, each one allowed to dry out before the next one is placed, with an extra layer of reinforcing straw or reeds between. When the walls are up and dry, holes for the doors and windows are cut out. Since the whole operation is done by eye without the benefit of any shuttering and because the corners are naturally weak, mud houses of this type have an undulating, rounded form like that of a well-fed pig. The finished walls were smoothed and then given an essential coat of lime-plaster rendering, regularly applied colour-wash or tar, which has the advantage that it stops cattle licking holes in the walls. The black tar can have sand thrown on to the top coat, so allowing it to be limewashed. This type of construction was common in the south-west of England, particularly in Devon, the south Midlands, the north-west along the Solway Firth, in Ireland, Wales and Scotland. The third type of construction only used in East Anglia, was clay bats, a technology introduced from Scandinavia or Germany. The blocks were cast in moulds, usually about 18 x 6 in. (450 x 150 mm) and made from a mixture of yellow clay and plenty of straw. They were left to dry naturally for up to a month and then built up in bonded courses using puddled clay mortar.

The fourth method, Pise de Terre, was rammed dry-earth walling requiring far more skill and was inherently more expensive since the process demanded shutter boards. The soil was pounded with a hardwood rammer until it became homogeneous. Its great advantage over the wet systems was that no drying time was needed and a full-height wall could therefore be built in a day. It was rarely used in England although common in parts of the Continent, not only because of the cost and skill required but also because it is difficult to get dry earth in our climate.

The most recent system, developed in the 1920s, was stabilised earth, in which a small proportion of cement was added to the mud which was then cast between the shutters as in Pisé. Alternatively stabilised earth could be cast in blocks using a special blockmaking machine. This system has only been used for a number of more or less experimental houses. Unfortunately it does not re-create the solid, comfortable, part-of-the-scenery look of simple mud. The present-day descendant of mud construction is concrete, a similarly free forming material.

Cob houses in Minehead, Somerset

1

2

3

1 An early 18th-century thatched cottage at Haddenham, in Buckinghamshire, near Aylesbury, built from wychert. This is a naturally occurring chalky clay found in an area south-west of Aylesbury extending about six miles in length by one mile in width. It conveniently appears about 600 mm (2 ft) below the surface. Mixed with straw and water it makes a good mud wall built in the same manner as cob. It is generally stronger, so the walls can be thinner, down to about 300 mm (1 ft) in thickness. Farther south in Berkshire, Hampshire, Wiltshire, Kent and Dorset a similar mix of chalk and clay has to be made artificially. Like cob, they all have to be plastered for protection.

2 A wall at Haddenham, with a pantile capping. At one time the village consisted almost entirely of wychert cottages connected by high winding wychert walls.

3 A detail of a wychert wall. Note the chalk stone foundation and the small fragments of chalk in the clay.

4 A group of early 19th-century cottages at Ashwell, near Royston, in Hertfordshire. Some cottages are built with clay bats, others with timber-frames covered with laths and left hollow. It is impossible to detect the difference between the two forms of construction except by tapping. Terraces are often built with the houses at the end of clay bat, with timberframe houses between, all covered with the same rough plaster and colour washed. Unlike cob, clay bats are usually thin, about 150 mm (6 in.) thick matching the width of a timber-frame wall. In the British Isles, its use was confined to the dryer counties, with suitable clays; East Anglia and the West Midlands, where Lye was known in the 17th and 18th centuries as Mud City. Clay bats were a much faster method of building than cob or wychert.

5 The window of an 18th-century cottage built of cob in Minehead, on the north coast of Somerset. The undulating form of the walls is created, not by subsidence or any form of collapse, but because they were constructed by simply placing the cob in layers, treading it down and then paring off the surplus. A simple operation often carried out by the building owner and his friends. The resulting walls were usually about 600 mm (2 ft) thick.

6 Clay bat wall. They are usually protected by plaster or tar from the weather.

4

5

6

57

4

5   6

1 16th-century cob manor house at Hayes Barton, near Exeter, in Devon. The base of the walls is stone. The plan is the traditional 'E' shape favoured at this period. The thatch is combed wheat reed, unbruised straw about a yard long, which is traditional in the south-west of England and makes a high quality roof that should last at least fifty years.

2 Early 19th-century cob cottage at Ashton, near Exeter, with a tarred stone plinth. Because of the time taken to lay the cob, a two-storey cottage like this might have taken two years to build. The appearance of many has been disguised by a recently applied skin of brickwork, stone or cement rendering.

3 Pair of cob cottages, probably designed by William Chambers, at Milton Abbas, near Blandford Forum, in Dorset, one of a number built about 1780 to form a carefully planned new village for a local landowner, the Earl of Dorsetshire. The roofs are of heather thatch with straw ridges. The two cottages share one entrance.

4 18th-century terrace of cottages at Melbourn, near Cambridge, partly built with clay bats: moulded blocks of air-dried clay, chalk and straw about 8 x 18 x 6 in. (200 x 450 x 150 mm) thick, much the same size as lightweight concrete blocks today. The outside walls are plastered and colour-washed. The walls rest on a base of tarred flint. The shutters are a late example of a type common in the Middle Ages.

5 A pair of 19th-century clay bat cottages in Shipham in the centre of Norfolk. The roof is covered with the pantiles typical of this county and the chimney stack is brick, since clay bat would not be suitable for use with coal fires. In earlier houses, using wood fuel, clay bats were used for stacks.

6 A pair of cottages by Edwin Lutyens and Alban Scott made about 1918 designed to use a variety of local materials depending on their availability. They could be built in cob, chalk or rammed earth. Many architects in this century, led by Clough Williams-Ellis during the 1920s believed that systems based on mud were highly suitable for low cost housing, so continuing an unbroken tradition dating back to before the Romans.   59

Building in stone

STONE HOUSES are much more difficult to build than timber, but stone has one great advantage: it is fireproof, a very important point when the chief reason for having a house at all in Britain was to keep the fire dry. The earliest stone houses date from about 3000 BC and were made from stone picked from the ground ('field stone'). At that time the stone areas of Britain would have been covered with loose stones and it must have seemed very convenient to clear the ground for crops and provide one's building material at the same time. In the far west and north of Britain, where trees were sparse, houses were built entirely of stone, the roofs formed of fiat overlapping stones continuing out of the walls till they met in the middle – a system used throughout Europe. The earliest houses were circular for three reasons: it was the logical shape to surround a fire, it followed the known pattern for timber houses of the period and, most important, it was very difficult to build a corner with odd-shaped stones used as they were picked up. The long house was developed when animals were introduced into the home both for their safety and to help keep the house warm in winter. The circular house was an inconvenient shape to accommodate both the family and cattle, but to build long rectangular houses in stone meant developing astonishing skills in selecting and placing stones together – so astonishing that it became the basis of the great tradition of secret craft societies for masons which have continued up to the present time. Even more astonishing is that houses of that period should have survived until today, complete with built-in stone cupboards and beds. In stone areas where trees were more plentiful timber was used for the structural supports, so the mason's skill was not so highly developed. Stone was used as a type of damp-proof course below a timber-framed wall and much later as a wall round a timber structure, when the owner could afford it as a protection against fire.

The walls had to be of enormous thickness – 2 to 3 ft (600-900mm) – in order to stand up without mortar – each stone being cunningly placed at a slight angle so that any moisture which penetrated or was driven in by the wind would run out. Holes were plugged with turves or smaller stones when available. The site for a long house was chosen with a slight slope, the animals at the lower end, so that there was natural drainage. The midden was kept safely indoors, since to those farmers it was like gold and the only insurance that their fields would continue to have good crops.

The Romans introduced quarrying and the technique for cutting stone to shape that made up for an increasing dearth of convenient field stone and also supplied stone in sufficient quantities for it to be transported commercially from areas of good supply to those without. For important buildings stone was brought from across the Channel but, except out of special necessity, ordinary houses used little stone until the 16th and 17th centuries when the available supplies of timber had been depleted by land clearances for farming, shipbuilding and fuel for industry. Local stone was still cheaper than brick which was only used for chimney stacks as it was more resistant to heat and easier to build with. Small quarries were cut wherever it was con- venient near to the building to save transport, the roads being appalling for heavy loads. All stone is porous to water and when first cut it is wet with quarry sap: a mixture of water and minerals. Most stones are then at their softest and easiest to cut. For this reason, as much work as possible is done at the quarry. After seasoning limestone hardens with a protective crystalline layer on the outer face left by the quarry sap on drying out.

Cut-to-size quarried stone meant an end to the corner problem, but the rest of the walls were usually filled in with loose stones bed-ded in mortar, often of much inferior quality and rendered. Fine grain stone could be cut and chiselled like wood but stone was not regarded with the same reverence as it is today: it was still simply the most expedient way to build a wall. Improved transport from the 19th century onwards made it possible to build Bath at Reading and Westmorland everywhere.

The British Isles are fortunate in having a great variety of building stone of all types, colours, and degrees of strength. Each quarry will produce not only a particular quality of stone but different parts of the quarry will give different qualities, all requiring careful study if the stone is to be used correctly.

All rocks can be placed into one of three major groups, namely igneous, sedimentary and metamorphic.

Igneous rocks
Igneous rocks are those which have formed by the solidification of molten rock which is called magma. Magmas originate at consid-erable depths within the earth's surface, and their temperatures are in excess of 600°C. ▶

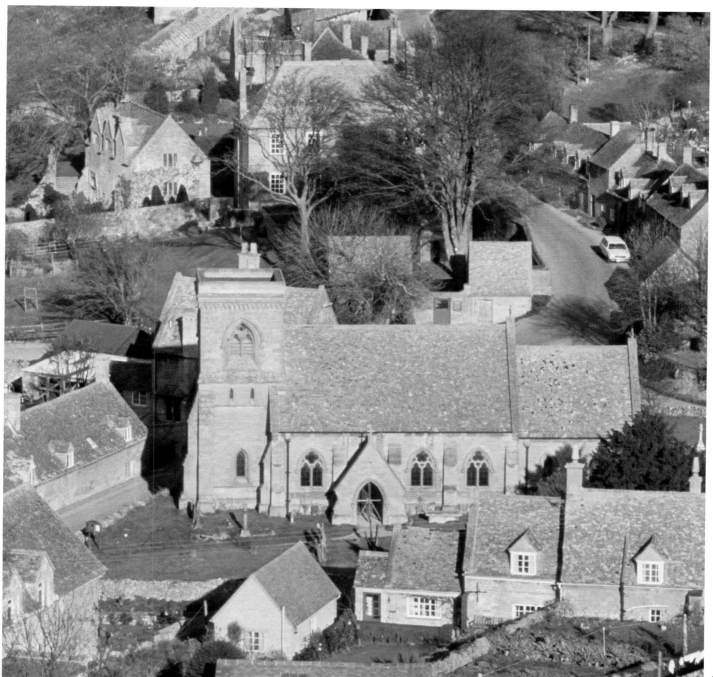

Cotswold stone village, Snowshill, near Cheltenham, Gloucestershire.

They can either intrude and become emplaced within other rocks, or they can reach the surface when they will form volcanoes and lava flows.

The characteristics of any igneous rock depend on several factors, the most important of which are the chemistry of the original magma, the length of time over which cooling and solidification occurred, and whether or not the magma assimilated the rocks through which it passed and thus altered its chemistry.

Igneous rocks provide some of the most durable building stones. They have good resistance to water and chemicals. In quarries they appear massive, although jointing can clearly be seen; this is the result of contraction within the rocks as they cooled when once solidified.

Until methods of cutting igneous rocks were rediscovered in the 14th century (the Romans not only cut but polished) they could only be used in the form of boulders, sometimes huge, which succeeding generations rearranged to suit their needs.

Classification of igneous rocks is based on two main characteristics: chemistry and crystal (grain) size. Rocks containing abundant quartz crystals are termed acidic, and those containing little or no quartz are termed basic. Furthermore, when magmas are intruded into other rocks, the surrounding rocks provide good thermal insulation and, in consequence, the magma cools and solidifies slowly. Such slow cooling promotes good development of individual crystals, and the resulting rocks are coarse "rained. Magmas extruded on to the surface are subjected to rapid cooling which permits only poor crystal growth and the resulting rocks are fine-grained.

Granite is an example of a coarse-grained acidic igneous rock which is emplaced at depth within the earth's crust and because of the erosion of the strata once lying above it the granite can now be seen at the surface. Its coarse grain, with crystals easily seen by the naked eye, gives it a pleasing appearance and it is among the most widely used of the igneous rocks for building purposes. One of the major minerals occurring in granite is felspar, which can vary from pink to white in colour, and such variations together with those of the other minerals present give each granite its own particular character.

Some granites, such as those of Aberdeen, are characterised by all the minerals having a similar grain size and therefore have uniform appearance. In contrast the granite of

Shap Fell, together with the granites of Devon and Cornwall, contain felspar crystals which are much larger than the other constituent minerals, and give the rock a less uniform and more interesting appearance.

Basalts are examples of fine-grained basic igneous rocks, and usually occur as lava flows. Contraction jointing has resulted in the spectacular outcrop of basalt which forms the Giant's Causeway of Antrim. Basalts are mostly quarried for roadstone.

The distinctive and attractive green building stone local to the Lake District is another type of igneous rock termed a tufa. During volcanic activity clouds of ash are often emitted, and when such ash settles out of the air onto the land surface, it can accumulate and eventually be compacted into a tufa.

Sedimentary rocks

Sedimentary rocks are essentially of secondary origin. Many of them originated directly from the disintegration of igneous rocks or of pre-existing sediments, but some are of organic origin and others were formed by chemical precipitation. The sediments were usually deposited on the sea floor and when first formed were in an incoherent form; their subsequent consolidation was brought about by pressure and by the deposition of cementitious matter through the agency of percolating water. A sedimentary rock is usually named after its main constituents; thus a rock consisting essentially of calcium carbonate is known as a limestone, one consisting ▶

1 Late 16th-century granite castle in Argyll.

2 Corner of a granite cottage in Co. Carlow, Eire.

3 Granite corner stones in a sandstone rubble wall in Cumbria. The slight set-back shows that the wall was originally plastered.

4 Granite dry stone cottage plastered, in Co. Wicklow, Eire.

5 Lyneham Hall, near Plymouth, in south Devon, built in pink granite in 1696.

6 Granite farmstead in Co. Wexford, Eire.

7 Sandstone house with granite corner stones in Fife, Scotland.

1

2

3

4

essentially of grains of sand as a sandstone. Sandstones and limestones are the principal sedimentary rocks which are used as building stones.

Sandstones

Sandstones are composed of the more resistant constituents of the igneous rocks and consist essentially of fragments of quartz with subsidiary amounts of other minerals, such as felspar and mica. The grains may be large or small, angular or rounded, closely packed together or less densely distributed in a matrix of other material. The most important feature of the sandstones is that the quartz grains themselves are relatively indestructible; their resistance to weathering is largely determined by the chemical stabil-

ity and cementing properties of the matrix material. The strongest sandstones are cemented together with silica, for example, the millstone grit of the South Pennines.

Limestones

Limestones consist essentially of calcium carbonate laid down as a sediment in water, deposited chemically from solution or derived either from living organisms such as corals, shells and other marine life which thrived in the shallow warm seas that at various times have covered parts of Britain. The loose uncemented particles were compacted and cemented together by the action of percolating water carrying calcium carbonate in solution.

5

6

Limestones are widely used as building stones because they can easily be worked, and within Britain there is a wide choice available, each with its own building properties and distinctive colour, the colour being created by various impurities such as iron.

Among the better known limestones of Britain are the Carboniferous Limestones of the Pennines which are hard, blue-grey and crystalline. Often they are very fossiliferous, containing many fragments of corals, sea shells and the stems of sea lilies. Its use as a local building stone accounts for the dour aspect of the houses in that area.

Although it has been said that limestones consist essentially of calcium carbonate, some limestones contain varying quantities of magnesium carbonate. Such limestones ▶

1 Limewashed late 18th-century cottages in Yorkshire built in limestone, with local millstone grit window and door surrounds. The roof too is millstone grit.

2 Terrace houses in Yorkshire built in 1698 using millstone grit.

3 Early 18th-century sandstone farmhouse in Bowness, Solway, Cumbria.

4 The windowless outer walls surrounding the farmstead of 3, designed partly as a protection against raiders from the North.

5 17th-century rendered sandstone longhouse in Cumbria. Some of the old stone flags can be seen above the gutter on the house part.

6 Sandstone walls of an old house, Cumbria.

65

1

2

are called magnesian or dolomitic limestones, and the magnesian limestone of
Yorkshire is widely used as a building stone.

Another type of limestone found in Britain
is oolitic limestone and consists of a mass of
small calcium carbonate spheres. These
spherical grains, or ooids as they are techni-
cally known, are formed by the precipitation
of calcium carbonate around a nucleus, such
as a shell fragment, in shallow, agitated seas
in tropical climates. The method of formation is similar to the formation of the scale
that will build up on small objects left in a
domestic kettle in areas using hard water.

The oolitic limestones provide some of the
best-known building stones, such as the yellow limestone of the Cotswold villages,

Portland Stone of Dorset, Bath Stone and the
Lincolnshire limestone of which the Ancaster
Freestone forms part.

The chalk, which forms the White Cliffs of
Dover, outcrops extensively in the southern
and eastern parts of England. Whilst, like
most limestones, it contains fossils easily
seen with the naked eye, chalk consists
essentially of a mixture of the minute skeletal remains of microscopic algae and of the
shell fragments of other microscopic organisms. Both skeletal and shell fragments are
composed of calcium carbonate which was
abstracted from the sea water by the living
organisms.

Chalk is normally white, easily quarried,
extremely easy to carve, but does not weath-

3

4

5

6

7

er well. It is often combined with brick or harder limestone at corners. An example of a harder limestone used in south-east England is ragstone, a hard, grey-blue, sandy limestone. Ragstone is brittle, difficult to shape, varies a great deal in character but because of a local shortage of hard stone it is much used in Sussex, Kent and London.

Flints, which occur within the chalk, are useful but difficult building material. They are irregular-shaped concretions and nodules of cryptocrystalline silica. The silica was leached by ground water from the sponge spicules which occur throughout the chalk and was later redeposited as the nodules known as flints. They are found in their natural curious shapes or rounded by the sea ▶

1 Late 18th-century sandstone farmhouse, cottages and barn in Cumbria. Note how each use is differentiated. The farmhouse has carefully cut corner stones and is set forward from the two other buildings.

2 19th-century sandstone house in Perth.

3 Millstone grit steps in Yorkshire.

4 19th-century street in a Yorkshire village. Practically all materials for walls, roofs and paving are varieties of sandstone. The blue Welsh slate roof is a recent replacement. Before the introduction of tar macadam, at the beginning of the 19th century, road surfaces like these were often of the same material as the surrounding houses.

5 Corner of an 18th-century sandstone house in Carlisle, Cumbria. The corners were originally exposed, the rest was rendered. The chisel marks originally cut to give the plaster a mechanical grip are now exposed.

6 Sandstone infill blocks at Avebury in Wiltshire. The chimney flues and gable end to the roof are constructed in brick, a far more tractible, as well as fire-resisting material than the sandstone locally available in the Marlborough area.

7 19th-century cottage near King's Lynn, Norfolk, using a variety of local materials: Snettisham sandstone, chalk stone, flints, brickwork with clay pantiles.

when they are similar to other loose stones which have had the same treatment. Over 80 mm they are called cobbles, under 80 mm (3$^{1}/_{2}$ in), pebbles.

Flints have been used for building since earliest times as they conveniently occur in areas without good natural stone, are easy to find, dig out and carry (the first mines were for flint). The strength of a flint wall depends on its mortar which has to bind the awkward ill-fitting shapes of the flints together. The Romans used excellent mortar, and since flints are virtually indestructible many of their walls still stand. Flint was not used for ordinary houses until the 16th century, when timber began to run out. It was often mixed with other materials: brick, chalk and tiles and then plastered over. As building standards rose, refinements only used previously for major buildings were introduced for houses. Flints were selected for size and arranged in courses, split (knapping), either on one face or into squares and placed in chequerboard patterns with other materials. Old flint walls have rounded corners, the new ones used stone or brick so they could be made square. Flintwork was very popular during the 18th and 19th centuries because of its decorative qualities. Today the craft has almost died out, but flint is extensively used as a facing material for precast concrete.

Metamorphic rocks

Metamorphic rocks were originally either igneous or sedimentary rocks and have been changed from their original form by the effects of heat or pressure or both. The heat and pressure may have arisen from move- ▶

1 Oolitic limestone in the Cotswolds showing the detailed carving possible.

2, 3 Imitation Cotswold stone (Bradstone) used today.

4 Market square at Castle Combe, Avon.

5 Oolitic limestone roof and walls near Bath.

6 16th-century tower house in Cumbria, built dry, using hard northern limestone.

7 19th-century cottage near Bath, built in smooth squared oolitic limestone.

8 Split limestone roof in the Pennines.

9 Typical whitewashed farm in the Lake District; the roof is local slate.

4

5

6

7

8

9

ments of the earth's crust, the intrusion of igneous rocks or the deep burying of the rocks by superimposed sediments. The changes brought about depend both on the chemical nature of the original rocks and the conditions to which they were subjected. Some rocks are altered little mineralogically and merely assume a new texture, for example limestones turn to marble, deriving their colours from impurities, and sandstones turn to quartzites. In comparison clays, shales and igneous rocks may respond to temperature and pressure by forming new minerals, and these new minerals become so arranged as to give the metamorphic rock a foliated appearance similar to that of tightly packed leaves of leaf mould. If this foliation is closely spaced and the rocks can easily be split into small pieces, the rock is termed a schist. Schists are usually named after the major minerals occurring in them, of which mica is one of the most common. In some metamorphic rocks the foliation is more open and often discontinuous, and such rocks are called gneiss.

Roofing slates, of which those quarried around Snowdon are famous, are metamorphic rocks. The original rocks were subjected to great pressure such that the constituent minerals were re-aligned along definite and parallel planes. It is along these planes that the slates can be so easily and perfectly split.

A great many metamorphic rocks, because of their hardness, are quarried for roadstone.

1

1 Chequer-pattern brick, flint and stone cottage near Salisbury.

2 Brick width chalk stone in Sussex.

3 Knapped flints and chequer-pattern brickwork near Reading, Berkshire.

4 Carefully sized pebble wall in Aldeburgh, Suffolk.

5 Mixed brick and chalk at Brancaster, Norfolk.

6 Kentish ragstone.

7 Selected but unshaped flints in Sussex.

70 **8** Dry slate walled house near Powys.

2

3

4

5

6

7

8

1

2

3

4

5

6

7

1 A typical stone hut of the 15th and 16th centuries much used by poor farmers all over Britain. It was the latest development of a house type originating in the Stone Age. The short roof ridge is supported by two vertical poles around which a number of branches are leant to form the roof. The covering consists of woven twigs with sods on top. The low wall is made of loose laid dry stone.

2 Conical circular stone house of a type used in the west of Ireland, most of Wales and in Scotland, Caithness and the Orkneys. Similar constructions are found attached to farms on Dartmoor. The stones are laid flat, without mortar, overlapping towards the centre, the top covering often being a sod.

3 A rectangular stone house in Inishmurray, Co. Sligo, in north-west Ireland. It is a variation on the conical type **2**.

4 Small l9th-century farm in Mallow, Co. Cork, in south-west Ireland, with stone walls smooth plastered with panels of rough cast. The roof is tripped and covered with reed thatch.

5 Small l9th-century limestone cabin at Bealaclugga on the edge of the Burren in Co. Clare. Normally the front would be painted white, the sides left unpainted. The roof is reed thatch, with stepped gable ends.

6 Hebridean black house, a type of long house that has been in use for two thousand years or more. The walls are about 6 ft (1800 mm) high and wide, with an earth core and dry stone outer skins. The corners are rounded. The roof is thatched with straw, reed or heather and held down with weighted ropes. The top of the wall is grassed.

7 l9th-century farmhouse just south of John O'Groat's in Caithness. The walls and roof are built of the same ancient sandstone.

8 Boothby Pagnell manor house, built in local limestone about 1200, near Grantham, in Lincolnshire. It has two floors, the upper lone with a fireplace. The original access stair was timber. The large central window was added in the 15th century.

9 Nursted Court, near Gravesend, Kent, built in the 14th century in local flint with imported Caen limestone dressings for corners, windows and doors. The roof is local sandstone.

8

9

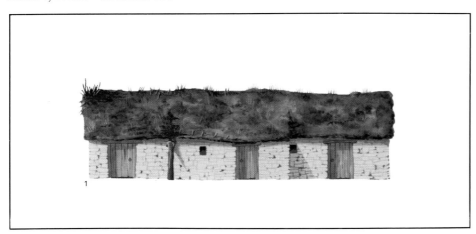

1   Medieval long house at Strata Florida, near Aberystwyth, in Dyfed, Wales. The roof is supported by a combination of curved branches (crucks) and upright poles supported on the ground; the walls, made of rough stone plugged with peat or turves, are only screens. The outside is painted pink, a traditional colour in Wales. The walls have no structural purpose. The roof is covered with small plaited branches under a layer of sods. The windows have no glass, the doors are made of unhewn logs. This farm was still inhabited in the late 19th century, but has now been demolished.

2   17th-century farmhouse near St David's in Dyfed on the south-west tip of Wales. The round chimney stack and large projecting fireplace are unique to this part of Wales, parts of the Lake District, north Devon and Somerset. These chimneys were introduced by the Normans; and conveniently solved the problem of how to build with small stones without shaped corners. The projecting stone fireplace dates from medieval times when the rest of the house would have been wood. The house is aisled, another Norman innovation, with a thatched section in the centre and shallower sloping sides covered in slate.

3   Early 18th-century farmhouse near Borrowdale in Cumbria. A development of the long house still built as one unit, but with the animals completely separated by an internal cross wall.

4   Early 17th-century farmhouse on Dartmoor in Devon. A development of the long house with the animals and family separated by a cross passage entrance for the animals.

5   An 18th-century farmhouse at Llanerfyl, near Welshpool, Powys, in Wales. The walls are dry stone, the roof supported on crucks and thatched with rushes with a turf ridge. A development of the long house with a solid dividing wall between the animals and family. The hearth is central, with a thatched chimney.

6   Ornamental gate lodge with stone walls and roof designed by Peter Robinson in 1823. He believed strongly in the use of local materials and traditional design.

7   A house built in 1966 near Cromer in the north of Norfolk using re-dressed stone from demolished buildings. The roof is covered with random-coloured concrete slates. It was designed by Stanley Warrell.

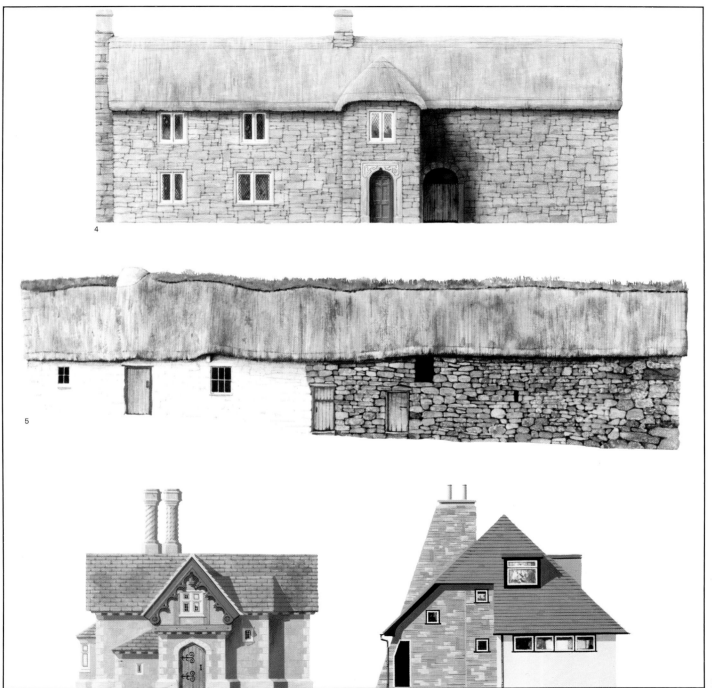

4

5

6

7

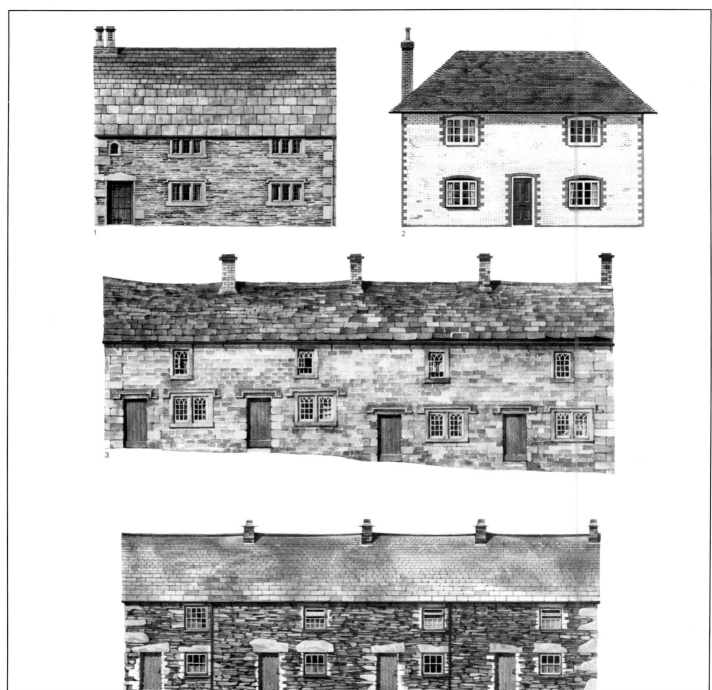

1 Late 17th-century farmhouse, Yew Tree Farm, Samlesbury, near Preston, in Lancashire. A simple but very well built three bedroom house with kitchen and living room on the ground floor; the plan is much like that of a small house today. The walls and roof are local sandstone, the mullioned windows have leaded lights. Now demolished.

2 Early 19th-century cottage in South Harting, near Chichester, in West Sussex. Built in local chalk stone with brick corners and a clay tiled roof. The windows are timber casement. This is a very typical design, also built in brick, flint, local stone and found throughout the south and south east of England. It was cheap to build, practical and simple in form, qualities that assured its popularity. It also reflects the elegant proportions of the classical designs of the 18th century. (See 2, p 70.)

3 Early l9th-century cottages at Winster, near Matlock, in Derbyshire. Built in local limestone, smoothly cut into blocks to form ashlar. The windows are Gothic-shaped cast-iron in mullions, a style that never quite died out in the North and so never needed reviving as in the south of England.

4 Early l9th-century cottages at Elterwater, near Ambleside, in Cumbria. The walls are of slate with uneven grarute slabs over the doors and windows, and at the corners. The lower windows are sliding sash, the upper windows, above the passersby, have cheaper horizontally pivoting upper halves, all designed to look the same. The roof covering is of evenly graded slate, the smallest at the ridge. The chimney flues are each protected by a pair of slates leant together.

5 A town house in St James's Square, London, designed by Robert Adam about 1775, who said of it 'where variety and grandeur in composition cannot be obtained we must be satisfied with a justness of proportion and an elegance of style'. Constructed of finely carved Portland stone, it is interesting to compare its enormous size with the cottages on the opposite page, in view of the quote. Robert Adam is the most famous of three brothers who practised architecture, interior design and speculative building together. Sons of an important Scottish architect, their influence can be seen in every town in Britain, a result of their combined genius for design and business acumen.

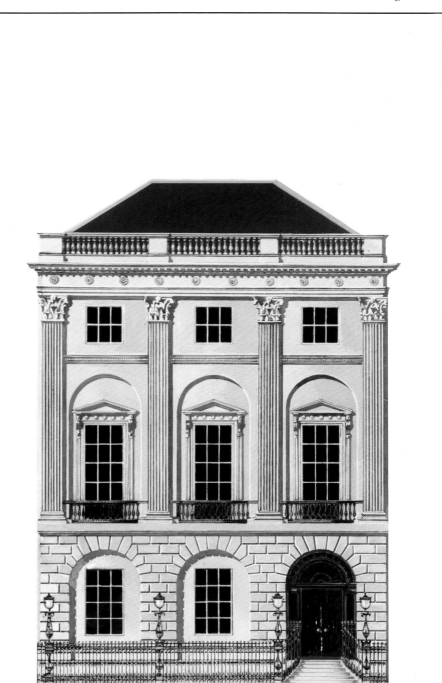

5

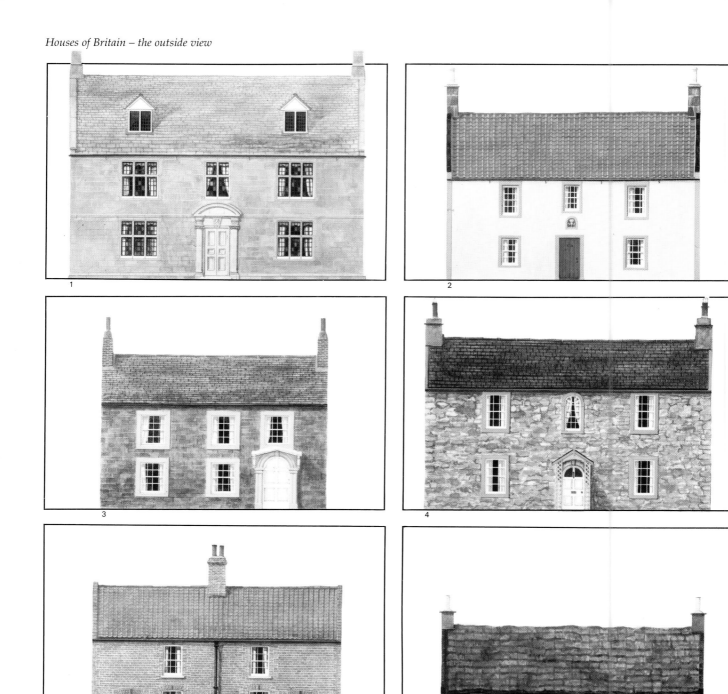

7

1 Merchant's house in Blockley, a Cotswold village in the north-east of Gloucestershire. Built in 1732, it has no cornice along the top of the wall and retains the mullioned windows and leaded lights typical of the previous century. But the entrance is classically correct, just what would be found on a fashionable London house of the same date. It demonstrates how difficult it sometimes is to date houses in the country which may be many years behind the major centres in current design. The walls and roof are Cotswold limestone.

2 Merchant's house in Airth, near Falkirk, Scotland. Built in 1730 of rough sandstone blocks covered with rough-cast plaster (harling), only the corners, windows and door have smooth stone facings. The roof is pantiled with stepped gables. This was a very popular house type, first introduced to Scotland around 1700, used by merchants, ministers, master craftsmen and small landowners – hence they are often called 'laird's houses'. The much colder climate of Scotland is reflected by the provision of small windows compared with the house at Blockley, **1**, built in the south of England.

3 Early 18th-century farmhouse built as part of a fortified farmstead at Bowness on the Solway, near Carlisle, in Cumbria. Built in squared red sandstone with a Westmorland slate roof the design is only approximately classical but has great strength.

4 Early 18th-century farmhouse in the fells near Caldbeck, built in rough sandstone with smooth stone facings to the windows and door. The roof is Westmorland slate. The arched window is commonly used in Cumbria for staircases and landings, as this example. Houses of this type, used throughout the north of England, often had leaded lights originally. The porch is a 19th-century addition, pretty in itself but masking the dour strength of the circular-headed door and its relationship with the circular headed window above.

5 Pair of cottages in Norfolk, just outside King's Lynn. Early 19th-century, built of local Snettisham sandstone, the only hard building stone in the county, with brick corners, window and door surrounds. The roof is covered with locally-made pantiles. These are often glazed a glossy black.

6 19th-century village house in Fife built of squared red and buff sandstone. In this case the red sandstone has been blackened to accentuate the wild design of the stone work. The roof is covered with sods, under which is a sleeping area above the main living space. In this case it is not lit, but in later houses or where improvements have been made, the roof is provided with dormer-windows, often with angled side windows for a view down the street, in towns. This house type is widely distributed both in towns and in the remotest parts of the Highlands of Scotland.

7 Old Hall Farm, Youlgreave, near Matlock, in Derbyshire, built in 1630, for a rich sheep farmer. It was built of coursed limestone with millstone grit sandstone corners, window and door surrounds. The chimney is red sandstone. The roof covering is sandstone tiles. It has a medieval plan then still popular in the north and north-west of England: there is a large hall divided by a central chimney stack opposite the entrance door opening to a kitchen and living area. At one end is a cross-wing with a parlour and buttery. Bedrooms and storerooms are above. The windows have leaded lights.

Building in brick

ALTHOUGH BRICKS have been used for important buildings since prehistoric times, it was only in the 15th century that they began to be preferred for ordinary houses. They offered a unique combination of fireproofness, durability, beauty of weathering, ease of handling and were increasingly competitive in cost in areas where timber and stone were in short supply. They have now become universal. The earliest bricks were earth blocks dried in the sun (see Building in Mud, page 54). They became the first man-made building product a discovery easily made when examining the remains of a burnt-out mud house. Suitable clay loams for brick-making have been deposited all over Britain. The different coloured bricks made from these earths depend on the minerals present, the method of firing and any other additives such as sand. It is the iron content of brick earth that makes brick reddish. When there is a lot of iron, the bricks are an intense bright red (Lancashire) or even go blue when burnt at very high temperatures (Staffordshire). Brown bricks contain plenty of lime but little iron (Humberside). Yellow bricks contain some chalk (Thames Valley) or sulphur. White bricks (Sussex and East Anglia) and grey (Oxfordshire, Berkshire and Hampshire) contain lime but no iron. Black bricks (South Wales, Surrey, Sussex and Berkshire) contain manganese.

The earliest bricks were made by the Celts who were not able to bake them to high temperatures so they were soft and fragile; by now they have largely gone back to the earth from which they came. The Romans introduced a much better product (still manufactured in parts of Italy) made in many sizes but typically 1 x 18 x 12 in (25 x 450 x 300 mm). These were thin so that they could be thoroughly fired and were known as wall tiles. The Romans made them by digging the clay in the autumn, leaving it all winter to be broken up by rain and frost and then kneading it in spring to remove any stray stones which would affect firing. The mixture was then beaten out flat on the ground and cut to size. The blocks were left to dry for anything up to two years for a top quality wall tile and then placed edgeways in kilns to be fired by wood. It was a lengthy, expensive process and ordinary houses in Roman Britain continued to be built in timber and mud, both readily available and cheap.

After the Romans left, there was a long period when no large important buildings were needed, and the craft was neglected. But the wall tiles themselves were not. Their qualities were highly prized and old Roman buildings were used as quarries whenever a particularly strong corner or foundation was needed up until the 16th century, when brickmaking again became widespread. Brickmaking on the Continent came back into favour about the 11th century and after the Norman Conquest, when major building projects started again, large quantities of bricks were imported from Flanders. Small quantities (particularly Dutch since the 16th century) have been imported ever since. They were also brought across as ballast in empty wool ships returning to the ports of Hull and Ipswich from their related Hanseatic ports in North Germany and the Low Countries. Brick ballast later accounted for many brick buildings in Ireland, North America and the West Indies. Brick became the fashion for the rich, many of whom lived and fought in brick castles in France; the word brick comes from the French 'brique', as do the chequer and diaper patterns popular in the Middle Ages and revived in Victorian times. It was a practical fashion in areas like East Anglia already short of timber and without much good building stone.

The first English bricks were made about 1200. They were made in moulds, not cut like Roman wall tiles, about 12 x 6 in (300 x 150 mm) and between 1¾ and 2¾ in (45 and 70 mm) thick, and continued to be made until the beginning of the 16th century. They were called Great Bricks. The Flemish immigrant craftsmen, sending along the east coast in the 13th century, were quick to introduce their methods of brickmaking. Flemish bricks were smaller and, like the modern brick, were designed to fit a man's hand comfortably, to speed laying. They varied from 8 to 9¾ in (200 to 250 mm) long by 3¾ to 4¾ in (95 to 120 mm) wide by 1¾ to 2½ in (45 to 65 mm) thick. The Flemish used a mould instead of cutting. Theoretically, this should have meant that the bricks made in one lot were of a constant size but because bricks were sold by number, not weight, the moulds were not completely filled, so they varied in size. Because of this, brick sizes were regulated by law in 1571 to be 9 x 4½ x 2¼ in (228 x 114 x 57 mm), a neat geometric proportion. They were called the Statute Bricks – to differentiate them from Great Bricks.

The early brickmakers travelled around the country making and laying bricks to order. They searched out pockets of local earth near where they were to build. Many villages have a humpy place called a 'brick ▶

The Mill at Elstead, near Farnham, Surrey

field'; many large houses have a pond which was once a clay pit. Bricks were fired in clamps; those at the centre were the best fired and were used for facing, the ones on the outside were least well burnt and were used for interior walls. The earliest-known building with English or Great Bricks is the Abbey at Coggeshall near Colchester, Essex (1220). The earliest-known building with Flemish bricks made in England is five miles away, Little Wenham Hall, near Ipswich, Suffolk (1275). Soon after 1300, there was a thriving brick industry in Hull, Humberside.

At first, brick was an expensive prestige material: it was moulded and cut into marvellous shapes to exploit its beauty, a tradition which lasted until the early 18th century (when stone and stucco began to be more highly regarded) and was revived in the second half of the 19th century. In small houses, the first use of brick was in the 14th century for the newly introduced chimney stacks. It was much easier to build with and more heat resistant than stone. Many stone houses have brick chimney stacks. As timber became more expensive and fire ravaged many old timber-built towns, including London, brick ▶

1 Mid 18th-century house in King's Lynn, Norfolk.

2 16th-century almshouse in Maple Durham, near Reading, Berkshire.

3 Chimney-stacks on East Barsham Manor, near Fakenham, Norfolk, built in 1525.

4 16th-century diaper-pattern brickwork in Berkshire.

5 Painted brickwork on a cottage in Kintbury, near Newbury, Berkshire.

6 Patterned brickwork on an early 19th-century house in Carlisle, Cumbria.

7 Early 19th-century Chinese bond on a cottage in Biggleswade, near Bedford.

8 Carved brickwork in a late 19th-century house in Brixton, London.

9 Flemish bond brickwork in a 19th-century house in Hertfordshire.

10 Chinese bond in a 19th-century stable building in Sussex.

2

3

4

5

6

7

8

9

10

1

3

5

6

came more into use, both on its own and with other materials like flint and rubble stone. It was also used to replace wattle and mud infill panels in timber buildings or for completely refacing them. Throughout this time most brickwork was in different shades of red, culminating in the magnificent bricks used by Sir Christopher Wren at the end of the 17th century, the finest period of English brickwork. The invention of the pugmill (a giant mincer powered by a horse) at the end of the 17th century saved beating out the earth by foot, and the introduction of coal-fired kilns in the 18th century led the way to more and cheaper bricks.

18th-century bricks had a fatter proportion – $2^{1}/4$ in thick x $8^{1}/2$ x 4 in (58 x 215 x 102 mm) because methods of firing had improved and it is quicker to build a wall with a thick brick. Between 1784 and 1850, brick taxes were imposed, with two results. First, there was a temporary increase in brick dimensions: bricks in the north are still traditionally larger than those in the south since at first bricks were taxed by number and not by size, and secondly there was extensive use of bricklike tiles on timber framework, and a revival of timber construction, mostly weather-boarded. Bricks in the mid 18th century were preferred in stone-like colours: white, grey and yellow, rather than the old reds which were considered garish. Mortar joints in brickwork were often coloured to match the bricks and then an even white joint was applied (tuck pointing) to give a smooth appearance. The Georgians were particularly fond of rubbed-brick arches over doors and windows that neatly related the fine woodwork to the irregular bricks. The arches were divided into narrow precise segments, usually red, with each brick made roughly to shape and then rubbed against another to its exact size. The joints are hardly discernible. Finally, in the early 19th century, brick buildings were stuccoed over with grooves to simulate stone jointing. The advantage was that poor-quality bricks could be used behind the rendering, but the upkeep in the dirty urban atmospheres of the period proved too expensive and around 1850, coinciding with the lifting of the brick tax and vastly improved methods of brickmaking, exposed brickwork returned to favour. Grinding machines replaced pug mills; mechanical pressing and wire-cutting, the old hand processes; and hot-air dryers, the sun. Bricks became exact in size, dazzling in colours ranging from every known earth colour to brown salt and a wide range of vitreous glazes. They were sent by rail to most parts of the country where they were cheaper than local produce. Only areas too remote, undeveloped or rich with stone were not affected: most of Scotland, southern Ireland, Cornwall, the Lake District, and the Cotswolds.

At the end of the 19th century some began to prefer the old hand-made bricks, starting a revival which meant that a few brickworks that had not become mechanised still survive. At the same time attempts were made to make mechanical bricks look like old ones but at less cost. These bricks were widely used for good-quality housing between the wars. The 20th century has seen the introduction of the most precise brick of all; cement and sand lime containing no clay, available in their natural greyish white or with various coloured pigments added. They have been widely used for low-cost housing ▶ 7

1 Early l9th-century house in Carlisle, Cumbria, with patterned brickwork, sandstone corners and stucco porch. The roof is slate from the Lake District.

2 Late 18th-century brick farmhouse in Berkshire. The windows and porch are not original.

3 Early l9th-century terrace cottage in Berkshire with variegated brickwork.

4 Late l9th-century cottage in Shefford, Bedfordshire, using Chinese bond.

5 First Rate House built about 1870 in Hurstpierpoint, near Brighton, East Sussex.

6 Pair of typical cottages built about 1900 near Guildford, Surrey. The front garden wall is local sandstone.

7 Late 19th-century terrace of artisan cottages in the North of England. The beautifully laid brickwork forms practically the only decoration. Note the traditional grained doors and window frames.

8 Pair of semi-detached houses in south London built about 1935. The brickwork is quite anonymous. Note how the new windows and door on the left-hand house have changed its character.

9 Modern house in Hampstead; the brickwork is treated like a sheet of solid material, the architectural emphasis is on the roof line and windows.

8

9

1

and whenever architects wanted, in an 18th-century sense, to express their buildings in shape and form instead of in the individual pattern and texture of the surface.

1   Manor Farm, Toseland, near St Neots, in Cambridgeshire, built about 1600. A late example of the Tudor style with the decorated chimney stacks, prominent gables and mullioned leaded windows typical of this period. The facings round the windows and door, also the horizontal mouldings and pilaster columns, are plastered to simulate stone, difficult to obtain in this area. The lacework of the leaded lights is an essential ingredient of the overall design, giving

human scale and delicacy to what otherwise is a severe design. The roof is clay tiled.

2   Mettingham Hall, near Lowestoft, on the borders of Norfolk and Suffolk, built about the end of the 17th century. A mixture of influences: Tudor scale, Dutch gables, Palladian door, all ingeniously combined together.

3   Hospital for Decayed Fishermen, Great Yarmouth, Norfolk, built as a group of houses for the retired by the town corporation in 1702. It is strongly influenced by the architecture of Belgium and Holland, with whom there was much trade at the time. The plain

shutters on the lower windows were then in normal use for small houses.

4   A three-bedroom cottage at Aldeburgh, Suffolk, designed by Oliver Hill about 1930. It carefully uses all the local traditions: a curvilinear gable in the East Anglian Dutch style with the angled 'tumbled' brickwork much used in this area. The roof is covered with black glazed pantiles and the walls are colour-washed, with a black plinth, all in the local vernacular. This approach to design, making the best use of local methods without undue regard to cost, was much in vogue between the wars amongst the more sensitive architects.

2

3

4

1

2

3

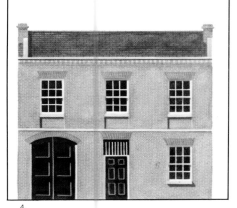

4

5

6

7

1   Eagle House, Mitcham, in south London, built about 1705 in the Dutch classical style introduced after the Restoration and perfected by Christopher Wren, Roger Pratt and others. It has the typical square plan of the period, derived from Palladio, but the tall, tripped roof, sloping down all round, the triangular pediment over the entrance, the massive symmetrically placed chimneys and the solid, heavily emphasised mouldings all come from Holland. The top of the roof is flat, covered with lead, with a way out from the house through a large cupola. This flat roof has a balcony and it was a favourite place from which to view the estate. The brickwork of this house is superb. The main windows have sliding sashes, introduced from Holland in the last half of the 17th century, but the basement and dormer windows are still leaded, as was usual at the time.

2   House in King's Lynn, Norfolk, at the end of a terrace, built about 1790, typical of many small brick houses in country towns of the south and east of England. The facade is basically extremely simple, with added adornment provided by the joiner : a decorated cornice below the parapet, a carefully formulated doorway.

3   Small town house in Winchester, Hampshire, built about 1800. More sophisticated than **2**, it shows the influence of Henry Holland, the most fashionable architect of the day.

4   Design for a First Rate house and its mews, published by Peter Nicholson in 1823. This was the largest type of terrace house in towns. Nicholson published a number of books of reference for architects and builders that have a great deal of influence.

5, 6, 7   Second, Third and Fourth Rate houses, also designed by Peter Nicholson and published in 1823. There is nothing very original about these designs: they are examples of the town-house types that had been developed throughout the 18th century and continued to be used with slight variations in style until the latter half of the 19th century. Their size, height and structure were all strictly laid down in building regulations according to their Rate.

89

1

2

3

Early brick walls were thick, laid with wide joints. They both became thinner as bricks became more even, because proper bonding was difficult to achieve with irregular-sized bricks. The first bond, called English (in fact it came from the French), consists of alternate lines of bricks laid end and sideways on. The weaker, more decorative Flemish bond (rarely used in Flanders) was introduced in the 17th century. It has bricks laid end on and sideways alternately in the same course. Another bond much used in the 18th century was header bond, where only the ends of the bricks are shown. The most common bond in use today is stretcher, where only the sides of a brick are shown. This is because of the universal use of cavity walls (first introduced in 1800) consisting of two skins, the outer only single brick thickness, which makes any other bonding system impractical.

Terracotta, a refined brick material used for mouldings, has only been used for short periods. First introduced around 1500 by Italian craftsmen the fashion lasted only a few years. It was revived in the 18th century, died out and was again revived at the end of the 19th century and in the early 20th.

Coade stone, another fine material was extensively used in the 18th century for intricate mouldings particularly around doorways. In the 19th century decorative glazed tiles were often used in porches.

1   Design by Gardner and Son for a Fourth Rate house and additions.

2   Design for two Third Rate semi-detached cottages by Gardner and Son.

3   Design for a pair of Second Rate houses by Gardner and Son.

4   Design for a 'First Class town mansion' by E. L. Tarbuck, in the 'ornate Italian style'. This was designed to be a brick house with cement rendering. A more expensive alternative could be built in stone.

All these designs come from a widely published book of designs and specifications much used by builders of the period: about 1860. It was called The Builder's Practical Director *published by James Hagger. It left nothing out.*

4

1

3

2

4

5

1 Design for a villa residence in the 'Rustic English Gothic Style' by Shaw and Lockington published in *Suburban and Rural Architecture* about 1860. The materials specified are red brick with Bath stone dressings.

2 Pair of semi-detached houses in Finchley, London, designed about 1910. The design is based on the 17th-century East Anglian cottage with a feeling for mullioned Tudor windows and thick Queen Anne window bars in places where they will not spoil the view. A speculative development.

3 Design for 'Old Scotch Lodge' in *Cottage, Lodge and Villa Architecture* by W. & G. Audsley, published about 1865. It was designed to be built in stone or red brick with a pale facing stone. The roof is slate to be 'in square, rounded or pointed slates, or in bands of slates of different shapes and colours'.

4 Part of a terrace of workers' cottages, designed in 1919 for a Midland industrial area by Corblet and Rose. A simple design derived from the 17th-century cottages of East Anglia.

5 Pair of semi-detached houses built in 1927 on the Beecholme estate near Clapham Common, London. Typical speculative houses of the period with cavity brick walls, rendered and pebble-dashed on the upper floor, with tile-hung bays and tiled roof.

6 End of a terrace of workers' cottages, designed by Cleland and Hayward in 1919 for a Midland industrial area. A very simple design, but unlike **4**, it is adapted from early 18th-century classical cottages, but without using the same system of proportion.

7 Detached house in Chislehurst, Kent, designed by Geoffrey Mullins about 1925. A carefully worked-out design following late Georgian styles. It is in no way a correct reproduction but it has assembled a number of decorative features borrowed from different periods.

8 Detached house at Braintree, Essex, designed about 1925 by Sir John Burnet and Partners. An early example of the international style in England and a return to simple geometry. The design has influences from current work in Holland and Frank Lloyd Wright in the USA.

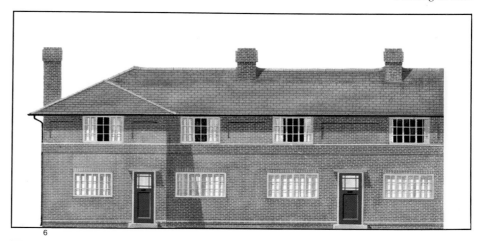

6

7

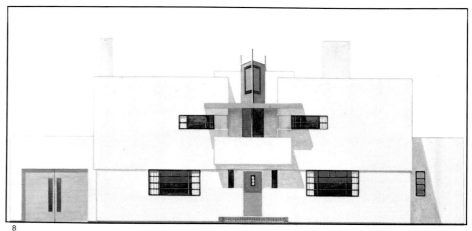

8

1 Early 19th-century brick cottage at Cardington, near Shrewsbury, in Shropshire. The colour-washed brick allows it to fit in gracefully with the surrounding stone houses. The windows, extremely subtly designed, are cast iron with hinged casements. The roof is covered in clay tiles.

2 Part of a terrace of workers' houses in Salford, Manchester, designed by Robert Austin for the Artisans', Labourers' and General Dwellings Company in 1869. This design, although for very low-cost houses, still manages to convey the impression of good craftsmanship.

3 Pair of semi-detached bungalows built speculatively in 1938 at Brighton, East Sussex. The corner windows, curved corners, horizontally barred maal window frames and sun-ray doors reminiscent of wireless sets of the period, are all carefully thought out with comfortable proportions.

4 A detached house, same period as **3**.

5 A popular type of detached house in the south of England, built about 1932. The roof is covered with green glazed pantiles, the walls are cavity brickwork with the smooth cement rendering that succeeded pebble-dash.

6 A pair of speculative semi-detached houses, built in 1960. Designed in the contemporary version of Regency style. They use the fashionable brown bricks and roof tiles now seen all over Britain, instead of the local red ones. The window frames are hinged casements, not sash, and the balconies are thin wrought iron, not the heavily decorated cast iron used in the late 18th and 19th centuries.

7 A detached bungalow built during the 1960s. The eyebrow dormer window in the roof with weather-boarding and leaded lights is very popular with speculative builders for giving a traditional distinction to an otherwise simple design.

8 Large detached house built in the late 1960s of simple design enlivened by a ten panel front door belonging to a Spanish, not British, 17th-century style.

9 Carefully proportioned Georgian-style house, built about 1960.

6, 7, 8 and **9** are all in one housing area just outside Hurstpierpoint, Sussex, and give an idea of the designs popular amongst speculative developers in the 1960s.

94

4 5

6 7

8 9

95

Rendering

RENDERING, OR PLASTERING, has been used from earliest times, first as a method of waterproofing and draughtproofing primitive constructional systems; its chief function being to plug up the holes, and later for its decorative qualities as well. The earliest rendering method was simply to spread clay over loose stone or wattle buildings. The clay was strengthened with cow hair and made more workable with dung and given a coat of lime-wash at regular intervals to protect it. This method of rendering was very common in all the clay areas of Britain down to recent times and many examples still exist in the West Country and East Anglia, more rarely in other parts.

An improved mix used at least since Roman times is known as daub, which was both stronger and more waterproof. This was spread on to the walls. An alternative method of applying a rendering, known as wet dash or harling, was throwing a mix on to the wall. This has the advantage of better adherence but results in a rough finish. Wet dash is common in the Celtic parts of Britain – Scotland, Ireland, Wales and Cornwall – whereas daub is more widely used in the Saxon parts. During the 13th century plaster of Paris was introduced and for a time was used externally because of its brilliant whiteness. It is, however, a very expensive material and it was soon felt that its use should be confined to interiors. However, the decorative qualities of rendering had now been recognised and it was used more and more for covering up inferior looking or mixed materials.

During the 16th century many skilful Italian plasterers came to England and plastering came to be used in a highly decorative manner in its own right with both mouldings and patterns drawn on the surface. This eventually led to the craft of pargetting, widely used during the 17th and early 18th centuries, particularly in the then rich eastern counties. It is reminiscent of the highly decorated ships of the day. It was revived at the end of the 19th century and is still practised today. As a style it owes much to German and Dutch influences through trade.

Palladio, the 16th-century Italian architect whose books had a fundamental effect on architecture everywhere, but particularly in England, used rendering over rough brick or stonework to give a homogeneous appearance to a building, so that the eye was not distracted by the individual bricks or stones of which the building was constructed. During the 18th century great improvements were made in the composition of rendering and towards the end of the century the early cements were first introduced, giving a much harder and more easily worked surface. This led to the wide use of rendering as a substitute for stone the surface being given a finish similar to smooth ashlar with stone course lines incised in the surface. At first these stone renderings, generally known as stucco, were simply colour-washed, but after about 1840 they began to be painted in oil, as this was more easily cleaned and the increasing pollution of the cities made this a very important aspect of exterior decoration.

The advent of early Portland cement in 1824 made an even more durable surface available and today nearly all renderings are Portland cement based. However, ordinary grey Portland cement on its own does not have a very pleasing colour and pebble-dash was introduced at the end of the 19th century to try and get over this problem. Pebbles are thrown on to the surface of the rendering whilst still wet the decorative quality of the result depending on their colour and size. The so-called Tyrolean finish is really a direct descendant of the wet dash or harling using a variety of coloured cements. The introduction of white cement during the 1930s has led to the development of new and extremely durable rendered finishes.

The visual quality of a rendering depends entirely on its final finish and many buildings have been restored with inappropriate finishes which have destroyed their architectural character. In a similar way, especially during the last century, many buildings which were designed to be rendered have had the rendering stripped in order to expose what was wrongly supposed to be the original construction. This is particularly true of half-timbered buildings. During the Tudor period and earlier, half timbering was generally exposed. When brick was introduced on a large scale during the 16th century, half-timbered buildings gradually came to be rendered in order to give them the same even quality of appearance as their brick counterparts. This meant that the timber work was often of a very uneven quality, as it was never meant to be seen. A similar problem has arisen with stone buildings, which were often built of loose rubble, intended for plastering, with squared corners and window surrounds.

16th-century house in Culross, Dunfermline, Scotland, faced in rough cast and colour-washed.

1

2

3

1 19th-century thatched stone cabin in Cashel, Co. Tipperary, Eire. Smooth rendered, grooved and painted to simulate painted ashlar stonework.

2 Late 18th-century rough cast stone farmhouse in Cumbria. The window surrounds are in stone, as is traditional in the north of England and Scotland.

3 Post second world war (1945) houses at Groomsport, Co. Down in Northern Ireland, of a type widely built by local authorities. They are finished in dry dash.

4 An early l9th-century terrace house in Brighton, carefully restored and painted to make the best of its classical design.

5 Unpainted cement rendering on an 18th-century house in southern Ireland The colour of the rendering has been carefully chosen to simulate the local grey stone. This is not the original rendering, but the lines imitating the stone courses do approximate to the original design.

6 Detail of 17th-century pargetting on a 15th-century farmhouse at Clare, near Bury St Edmunds, on the borders of Suffolk and Essex. (See drawing page 100.)

7 Beautifully executed, rustic-style rendering on a Gothic Revival cottage in Wiltshire. Note the way the elegant window opens, reminiscent of the watchmaker's art.

8 Detail of the superb stucco work carried out to the design of John Nash on a terrace house in Regent's Park, London.

9 A late 18th-century house covered in unpainted stucco. It spans a small backwater at Oxford, where natural stone is abundant.

10 Plastered cottage at Castle Combe, Avon, built in the 17th century. This is a practical way to deal with a potentially draughty timber-frame house; cover it all with plaster. Unfortunately, many of these houses have been stripped to expose the timber-frame that was never meant to be seen, extremely inappropriate in a village like this almost entirely built of stone.

11 1925 pebble-dash, a popular way of decorating houses at the time.

4

9

5

7

10

6

8

11

1 A 15th-century farmhouse at Clare, near Bury St Edmunds, on the borders of Suffolk and Essex. Pargetted at the end of the 17th century in floral patterns and originally with a fabulous winged monster which no longer survives. Pargetting is usually carried out on timber frame buildings. It consists of a thick, hard-wearing coat of plaster made from a mixture of ordinary lime, sand, cow hair, cow dung, chopped straw, urine and water. It can be applied on both the inside and outside surfaces of a wall. The decoration is modelled by hand or formed from moulds and templates. The simplest method is to incise a design, sometimes through to a layer below, using a pointed stick, comb, or a fan made up of a number of sticks. Typical designs are tortoiseshell, square pricked, zig-zag, scallop, herringbone, interlacing wavy lines, crow's feet, cable pattern, semi-circles, lozenges, scales, flowers, fan and basket. The zig-zag is common in Essex, scallop in Hertfordshire and herringbone in Suffolk. Although mostly confined to East Anglia, pargetting is also found in Kent, Buckinghamshire, Bedfordshire and Berkshire and as far away as York, the skill carried by itinerant craftsmen. The decoration was often picked out in colours, such as bright apple green, yellow ochre and the earth reds. Whatever the applied colours were, constant applications blurred the image and very few genuine examples of old pargetting remain. Most have been renewed a number of times since they were first carried out. Fortunately, this has served to keep this very old skill alive (the Guild of Pargetters was founded in London in 1501) and there are a number of highly skilled and imaginative craftsmen still working in East Anglia.

2 A pair of 17th-century cottages in Great Dunmow, Essex. These have timber frames, covered with laths both sides and plastered. The final coat is covered with very fine gravel, thrown on and then limewashed. This is not to be confused with early 20th century pebble-dash, which used a much larger stone and was not intended for painting when first applied. However, pebble-dash that has deteriorated after fifty years or so, is often now restored by the application of a suitable paint, the final appearance being not too dissimilar to the traditional gravel finishes of the past.

3 Late 18th-century sandstone cottages with plaster finish and local slate roofs at Hesket Newmarket, in Cumbria.

4 Design for a gate lodge by the Scottish architect John Starforth in 1890 and published in *The Architecture of the Park*; typical of many built at this period in stone or stucco. Since 1500 stucco has been regarded as a useful alternative to stone, giving much the same appearance, at least from a distance. It is essentially a smooth hard coating incised with the simulated outlines of stonework. At first satisfactory ingredients and mixes were rare and architects jealously guarded the secret of their recipes, however unsatisfactory. The secret of Coade stone, a form of artificial stone much used for moulded decorations in the 18th and early 19th centuries was so carefully guarded that the company making it finally lost the formula and had to go out of business. The Adam brothers had their own successful patented stucco and were responsible for its great popularity during the latter part of the 18th century. John Nash used stucco almost exclusively, the best known examples being his terraces in Regent's Park, London. It was extensively used throughout the 19th century, particularly for the basement areas and ground floors of town houses and for embellishing their window surrounds and parapets. It was much criticised at every period by purists, who preferred real stone and suspected that its true value was to cover up poor brickwork. The basic system was to apply two or three coats of sand and lime, the last smoothed with water brushed on and a wooden float.

5 Pair of semi-detached houses in a north London suburb, built in 1925. The walls are cavity brick finished with a pebble-dashed cement rendering and a brick plinth. The timber window frames have leaded lights and the front doors have small windows with the then popular rising sun also leaded. The roof is clay tiled. The design, based on 17th century cottages and their extensions, is restrained and carefully worked out.

6 Detached house in the Spanish style that has become fashionable in Britain as a result of the recent popularity of Spain as a holiday country. The same kind of thing happened when people from this country started to go to Italy on the Grand Tour in the 18th century. This house was built about 1965. The woodwork is oak, stained and polished. The windows are protected with wrought-iron bars, the brick walls are covered with white Alpine Finish, and the roof is covered with Roman pantiles.

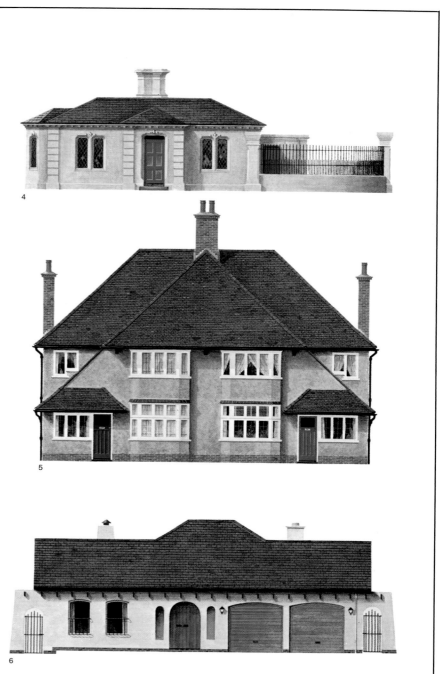

Modern methods

THE POPULATION OF BRITAIN, for centuries practically static, is now eight times larger than in the 18th century. More people now live alone and people live longer. This sudden increase over the past two centuries has created a continuing demand for homes that could not be met by traditional methods of building alone. They were too slow and need a high degree of craftsmanship and materials that were hard to come by in quantity. Quicker building methods were sought that ideally could use unskilled labour and new cheaper materials that could readily be bought in bulk. There has always been a degree of prefabrication even in traditional methods (the Pyramids were built with blocks cut and finished at the quarries and then transported to the place they were erected) but the first well organised systems started during the latter half of the 18th century.

This period also saw the appearance of the first developers, who, taking advantage of the standardised house types then current, were able to place large orders for components. Standard windows and doors were turned out by large joinery firms to a variety of well-designed patterns: it is easy to find identical 18th-century front doors in houses hundreds of miles apart. The technique of casting plaster and similar materials such as Coade stone also lent itself to quantity production. This was a much cheaper and quicker method of obtaining a similar appearance to finely carved marble, for a demand far greater than the number of carvers available could have met. At the same time the technique of casting was used for iron to simulate the expensive hand-wrought work that could not be created in quantity because of a shortage of skills.

These methods have been employed ever since: it is still possible to buy plaster mouldings cast from patterns made in the 18th century that were used by Robert Adam. Precast concrete, developed in the 19th century and now widely used in housing for roof tiles, wall blocks, paving slabs and lintel-beams over doors and windows, is an extension of the same principle, as is glass-fibre moulding, introduced in the 1950s and often used for decorative features.

The first fully prefabricated houses in this country appeared in the 1850s. They were made in cast iron and called Portable Houses but were meant for export to countries without building skills and not intended as a solution to Britain's housing shortage. It was not until lighter, more practical materials such as corrugated iron became widely available at the end of the 19th century that the prefabricated house in Britain became feasible. Army huts, particularly the Nissen, gave prefabrication a great boost during the First World War; many were re-erected afterwards as houses and were still giving good service fifty years later. After the Second World War, small completely equipped houses were made in steel, aluminium and asbestos cement.

The advantages of prefabrication are that most of the work can be carried out under cover, independent of weather, in factory conditions. The design can be refined to suit the most advanced production technologies so that the site work is reduced to the minimum and is largely unskilled. Site cranes introduced about 1950 have proved immensely useful. The disadvantages of prefabrication are the greatly increased management costs, the overhead cost of building a factory and servicing it and the cost of transporting large and damageable components to the site, unless the project is large enough to allow the factory to be built on it. Although in theory unskilled labour should be much cheaper than skilled this is not so, because unskilled work is extremely boring. This means that prefabrication can only be seen as an addition to traditional building methods, not as a substitute. The exception is the fully factory-finished house: the caravan.

To compete with traditional materials, any new product has to have distinct advantages for builders. It must be more readily available or quicker to use or cheaper or need less skill. Many have inherent advantages with which traditional materials cannot compete, such as lightweight concrete blocks and no-fines poured concrete that provide far more heat insulation than comparable stone or brick walls. The terrace house in Blackheath, shown opposite, demonstrates subtle combinations of new and old materials. The roof has a shallow slope and is covered with aluminium (good for heat insulation). The gutters and down-pipes are plastic and do not need painting. The windows are large with aluminium frames. Between the houses are solid machine made bricks for fire protection and strength. The outside walls are framed in timber with aluminium windows and traditional timber weather-boarding. The door is adapted from a standard wood frame with glass. The forecourt is paved with pre-cast concrete slabs. This was designed at a period in the last century when the ideas of designing for the time were held to be true.

The 1980s heralded another major phase of building in the British Isles. As much land as was built on in 1975 was built over again. Mostly, prime agricultural land. Major corridors of developments were made available for the volume housebuilder to build. During this period the architect's design skills, responsible for at least the pattern book, were hardly used and the surveyor and builder built for profit as before. The styles preferred ignored the modern technical tendencies of a decade before, avoided being contemporary and allowed planners and developers to built in neo-vernacular and foreign traditional styles. The design influences being re-imported from the US and the continent as system building.

Certain developments nevertheless try to retain a sense of the regional vernacular and provide a variation in the setting and variety of design, most of these are modelled on the vernacular aspirations of Poundbury a new town outside Dorchester. Local materials, such as flint peculiar to chalk areas, are used to replicate a local way of building.

Mass produced timber balloon framed two-storey dwellings in detached settings are familiar all over the country. The difference between inner city, suburban and rural is minimal since the preponderance of style is toward the developers' vernacular. Certain methods are reworked to produce a style particular to a certain time such as diagonal weatherboarding popular in the area around Cambridge from the mid-1980s.

The speed of construction available due to the use of prefabricated items is exemplified by the IKEA flatpack house of the 1990s which is supplied as a kit and is almost universal in application, bringing in homogeneity and an end to regional variation.

Experiments in straw bale, cardboard and greenwood construction are responses to a further economic twist brought about by the lack of certain resources. The economy of energy has always been an issue despite what the double glazing people say. Sustainability is traditional concern and it is the changing demands of society that invite new solutions.

It will be interesting to see whether the effect on the visual sense of the house builder and buyer is affected by the recent upturn in immigration and the effect of prefabrication being carried out under the different vernaculars of the EU.

Housing block 2001, Sutton, South London, using reclaimed materials

A recent concern in building is the ecological consequences of building. The houses shown above right are designed to reduce the impact on the environment by using recycled, reclaimed and renewable building materials. All the materials used are from local sources to reduce the energy used is transport. The houses are south facing with gardens on terraces so using less land and being able to benefit from the heat of the sun which reduces energy consumption. Sealed triple glazing units are used with large amounts of insulation made from hemp.

The timber cladding is green oak from local storm damage cut on site. The roof is planted with sedum, a drought resistant plant that harbours wildlife native to the site. Wind cowls on the roof ventilate the houses with air that is heated by the exhausted air.

Terrace house in Blackheath, 1964

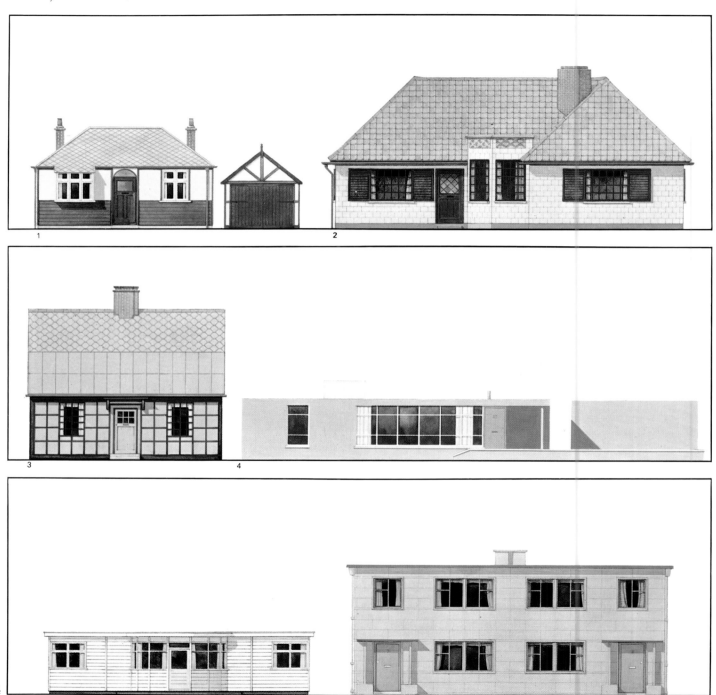

1

2

3

4

5

6

1 'My Heart's Desire', a popular cottage bungalow 'suitable for chauffeur, gardener, week-end or general use' made by the AMA Portable and Permanent Building Works in 1927. It is constructed with a timber frame covered with weatherboarding and asbestos cement sheets. The roof is covered with diamond-pattern asbestos tiles available in various colours.

2 Bungalow designed by Constantine and Vernon and exhibited at the Daily Mail Ideal Home Exhibition in 1923. Constructed with patent hollow concrete-block walls claimed to be quicker to build, lighter in weight, more economical in mortar, warm in winter, cool in summer and to 'endure for centuries'. The roof is of concrete tiles.

3 The grey 'Poilite' house designed by Henry Shepherd in 1919, a standard house to be built of brick or concrete and covered with a variety of asbestos cement sheets.

4 Single-storey house designed by Connell, Ward and Lucas at Bourne End, Buckinghamshire, in 1935. The walls are 100 mm (4 in.) thick reinforced concrete; the roof is a slab of reinforced concrete 125 mm (5 in.) thick, lined with insulation board. The windows are steel and the tubular vertical mullions carry the weight of the roof above.

5 The 'Sunshine' bungalow, designed and built as a fully-finished prefabricated product by Boulton & Paul in 1936. It is entirely made of timber on traditional lines adapted for factory production.

6 'Orlit' prefabricated semi-detached houses designed by Ervin Katona about 1945. The frame is reinforced concrete, the walls of concrete blocks.

7 A pair of semi-detached houses designed by Frederick Gibberd and Donovan Lee, in 1946. They have steel frames, corrugated steel first floors and non-load-bearing brick ground floors.

8 The Wates prefabricated house using precast concrete panels, designed to take six days to erect on a prepared site. The system was developed during the 1939-45 war.

9 Houses at Crawley New Town, designed by Phippen, Randall and Parkes in 1969. They are constructed in honey-coloured concrete blocks.

7

8

9

105

Chimneys, roofs and gutters

Chimneys The word chimney originally meant a fireplace. There was no such thing as a chimney in the modern sense and in the ordinary house the smoke was simply allowed to float up through the thatch or a small hole in the roof. Although the Romans had chimneys, the Saxons preferred the simple open fire in the centre of the house. The first improvement to this system was to provide louvres in the roof to prevent the rain getting in as the smoke got out. In simple houses these were made of wattle or thatch like the roof and examples were still in use in the Scottish Highlands in this century. More sophisticated methods in common use by the 13th century were the making of pottery or timber louvres, which were often highly decorative. Chimneys proper had been in use in great houses in the 12th century but the pressure to use them in small houses did not come until the introduction of coal as a fuel in the 14th century. Smoke from wood was bearable, but smoke from coal was intolerable. By the 15th century chimneys in London made of timber and mud had become quite common, the fireplace having been moved against the end wall, although plaster, stone or brick were preferred. By the end of the 16th century most houses had a chimney stack of some kind, but many small houses in the country were still without a proper brick chimney in the mid 18th century. These early stacks not only served the fire that warmed the house but were also used for cooking and smoking bacon. They had to be big enough for a boy to go up and clean them. Great pride was taken in their design and each area had its own vernacular. Chimney pots, whose function is to improve the flow of air, were in use as early as the 13th century, but their general use only started in the middle of the 18th century with the introduction of tortuous flues to serve every room in the house.

Roofs The word thatch originally meant any roof covering but because the majority of roofs were covered in either straw, reed or heather its meaning has become limited. The earliest houses could be considered to be all roof, the 'walls' being formed by removing the top soil so that the floor of the dwelling was well below ground level (a tradition which persisted until the 18th century). The roof construction consisting of branches was then covered with available vegetable matter mixed with earth such as grass sods, twigs, heather and moss (moss was still being used for sealing tiles in the 19th century). These roofs were too fragile to last more than a season and they were often stripped off and used as fertiliser in the fields, the soot deposit from the fire inside making them even more suitable for this purpose. Stripped of its covering, the roof was extremely portable and the tradition that the roof belonged to the tenant like his furniture, while the more solid walls belonged to the landlord, persisted in Ireland and Scotland until the last century. Another ancient tradition going back to Celtic times, or possibly even earlier, was the setting of the figures of birds, usually formed in straw, at each end of the roof. This idea has come down to modern times in the decorated tile finials of the 19th century. Since roofs are sloped to shed rain, it is quite logical to find that very thin or small sized materials such as thatch have the steepest slopes (up to 75°) and the homogeneous ▶

1 A 19th-century stone cabin overlooking Galway Bay in west Eire. The thatch is reed and the gable end walls are stepped; a simple device for avoiding the complication of cutting stone at an angle.

2 Wheat straw thatch on an 18th-century cottage in South Harting, near Chichester, in West Sussex.

3 Limestone tiles on a porch at Calne in Wiltshire. Note the way they are graded from top to bottom.

4 Limestone tiles on a stone cabin in Milton Malbay, Co. Clare, near the coast in the west of Eire. The joints are filled with lime.

5 A complete slate house built in a slate quarry at Llanfrothen, Gwynedd, in North Wales, as a monument to the decorative art of the Welsh slater.

6 Traditional pantile roof first introduced from Holland in the **17**th century and much used in the east and north of Britain, as well as Somerset. This example comes from a black weather-boarded cottage in Essex.

7 Plain hand-made clay tiles on a 16th-century timber house in south Berkshire.

8 A Victorian farmhouse in Hertfordshire with mass-produced clay tiles and decorative bargeboards – a vital part of the design of the house.

9 Machine-made concrete tiles on a bungalow built in Sussex in 1974. The regular geometric shapes and hard shadow lines give these roofs a distinctive character.

materials like metals or roofing felt can be laid practically flat: each material has its own ideal angle. One can easily see how many buildings used to be thatched by the extreme steepness of the roof, although they may now be covered with tiles.

The plan form of a house was largely dictated by the roof construction: by the available length of tie beam to hold the rafters together. This accounts for so many old houses being the same size. Large square houses could only be built by using an internal gutter- something which would be impossible to use with a thatched roof because the thatch would rot. An alternative, much used for classical houses, was to have a lead flat roof spanning between the two ridges (often developed into a viewing platform). Single-storey extensions to two storey houses, usually for butteries or outhouses, were made by continuing the roof down along one or more sides of the house. The earliest houses had tripped roofs: the roofing continued all round like a bell tent. It had particular advantages when the walling method was weak and could not be built high. Gables, where the wall is taken up to the full height of the roof at the ends of the house, allow the house to be easily extended lengthwise and are particularly suitable for terraced town houses where the rain water can be discharged to the front or back but not at the ends. They are also much more suitable for stone or pantile roofs, which are difficult to manage except in straight runs. Because roof space is valuable, tripped roofs generally have steeper ends than sides to give more room. This is easy to accomplish in a flexible material like thatch but difficult with tiles because the courses get out of line. The solution is the tripped gable, where the angle can be the same all round. The flat roof has none of these problems.

Apart from green moss and sods, much used in Britain until the 19th century, a variety of materials is used for thatching. Reed thatching is the best and is the traditional material used in East Anglia. It is usually about 6 in (150 mm). thick and should last eighty to a hundred years. Straw thatch, using either wheat, barley, oats or rye, introduced in the 19th century when the corn became long enough, has to be much thicker – about 15 in (380 mm) in order to be waterproof. Whereas reed thatching is a professional craft the advantage of straw thatching was that it could be carried out by farm workers used to thatching haystacks. The best straw thatch, rye, has a life of about thirty years. Other forms of thatch are sedge, broom, heather, bracken, flax, combed wheat, reed and long straw. Thatched roofs have no gutters and roof angles very depending on the relative importance of rain or wind from 60° to 75°. Where gales are particularly fierce, as in the west of Ireland and the north of Scotland, thatched roofs are tied on to the houses or have weighted ropes thrown over them. The traditional method of protecting thatch roofs from fire was to whitewash them, a custom which still persists in parts of Wales, and now applied to slate roofs. The special quality of thatch is the great insulation it provides.

Another ancient roof covering is shingles (wooden tiles) widely used in Roman times and up to the 15th century, when the high cost of timber made them generally uneconomic. However, they were still being used in the 18th century. They were made from oak, about 2 ft (600 mm) in length by 7 in (175 mm) wide, and laid with an overlap of about 8 in (200 mm). The lower end was thicker and either rounded or pointed to throw the water away from the joints. They made a light, durable roof (lasting fifty to a hundred years or more) weathering to a beautiful silver grey, but they had the disadvantage like thatch of being flammable. Today, Canadian western red cedar can be supplied at much less cost.

Apart from thatch and shingles, the only other naturally occurring roof covering is stone, which has the advantage of being non-flammable. The disadvantage in early times was that the slabs were heavy and unless they were self- supporting (in the manner of a beehive hut) any supporting structure of timber had to be extremely strong. The Romans used hexagonal slabs of stone secured with hand-made nails. Stones suitable for roofing have to be easy to split in one direction, such as certain sedimentary lime – and sandstones and slate. Although slate can be split in almost any thickness, sedimentary rocks can only be split in comparatively thick layers. As a result, they are much thicker and so heavier, which usually means a steeply sloping roof of 50° or more to stop the rafters bending. Stone flags are large and heavy, up to 4 ft (1220 mm) wide and 3 in (75 mm) thick. Stone tiles are much lighter and thinner. They are traditionally laid in graduated sizes – the largest at the eaves, the smallest at the ridge, in order to reduce weight – and waterproofed with moss laid between the joints and a mixture of clay and hair applied to the underside. Each tile or flag was drilled and fixed by a ▶

1 A pair of highly decorated brick chimney stacks on a timber frame house at Brent Eleigh, near Bury St Edmunds, in Suffolk, built in the early 17th century. At a time when most houses were timber, the chief occupation of the bricklayer was to build chimney stacks, still an innovation at this time for smaller houses. They naturally took great pride in their design and construction.

2 A brick stack set at an angle; a subtle way of relating a tall square stack to the triangular shape of the roof. Much used for cottages from the 18th century onwards. This example comes from a thatched cottage in Southill, Bedfordshire.

3 The numerous fireplaces in tall Georgian terraced houses lead to simple slab stacks penetrated by numerous, often tortuous, flues. Chimney pots were introduced to smooth the outflow in an attempt to make them as efficient as the older single and double stacks with large straight flues. These examples are in Bath, Avon.

4 A group of thatched mud cottages with brick flues plastered to match the walls in Selworthy, near Minehead, in Somerset.

5 One of a pair of octagonal brick chimney stacks on a farm in Bedfordshire. The design has been as carefully worked out as if they were a pair of silver candlesticks (which they greatly resemble).

6 An 18th-century stone chimney stack on a cottage in north Devon. The round stack was introduced to Britain by the Normans who found it convenient in areas where the local stone was difficult to square for corners. (See 2, page 74.)

7 Down draughts and therefore smoky chimneys can be caused by adjacent high buildings. or trees. The cure is to heighten the stack, but in this example in Kent the tree has long since been cut down.

8 A typical four-square 18th-century chimney stack near Leatherhead, Surrey, provided with projecting brick courses to afford weather protection to the main body and a degree of decoration.

9 A pair of Victorian chimney stacks near Reading, Berkshire, designed in memory of the great days of the Tudors.

1

2

3

4

5

6

7

8

9

109

peg of oak or sheep's bone to the rafters. Early slate roofs were laid in just the same way, but because they were thinner they could be laid on roofs which were less steep. The thin Welsh slates which became popular at the end of the 18th century, can be laid to pitches as low as 30° because of their large size and lightness. Small slates need a slope of at least 45°. The popularity of slate depended upon two qualities: first, the supporting timber work could be light and was therefore cheap and, second, it was conveniently unobtrusive for classical-style buildings which otherwise had to have expensive lead. The life of a slate roof is at least a hundred years; it is the iron nails used to hang the slates which give way first.

For a roof which is as non-flammable as stone, as light as thatch and which can be laid at any angle, lead is the answer. The only difficulty is that it has always been extremely expensive. Used by the Romans and Saxons for very costly buildings, it was not generally employed for houses until the 15th century, and even then only by affluent individuals. Since lead has a tendency to creep and slide, on steep slopes it should only be used in small sheets. Medieval plumbers used much narrower, shorter and thicker sheets of lead than were common in the 18th and 19th centuries, and they lasted a great deal longer. Lead has a life of about a hundred years before it decays into pinholes and needs stripping. Alternatives to lead are copper, aluminium, zinc, asphalt and bitumen felt. None of these has as long a tradition in British building and so they possibly may be ruled out on the grounds of appearance, copper turning a bright green and aluminium never quite losing its bright silver colour. Zinc is cheap but has a short life. The appearance of asphalt and bitumen felt cannot compare with metal roofs.

There are two kinds of tile, the plain, flat tile based on the flat oak shingle, which it replaced as being more fireproof, and the pantile, which is a development of the Roman system. To start with, tiles were very expensive, though cheaper than lead; and were used in place of stone in areas like London and the south-east of England where this was not easily available. Plain tiles, the first to be reintroduced are about $10^{1}/_{2} \times 6 \times {}^{1}/_{2}$ in. (267 x 150 x 12 mm) and slightly concave so that the water is directed away from the joints. They are hung from light timber battens on pegs, like stone tiles, or by nibs, moulded onto the tile. Each tile laps two others (called treble-lap) leav-

ing only about 4 in. (100 mm) exposed with a roof slope of 45° or more. Unlike stones or slates, clay tiles have regular, rather than diminishing, courses but they vary slightly in size when hand-made; they should be laid as they come, never sorted out into regular lines. Improved manufacture in the 17th century made them cheap enough to compete with thatch. Pantiles which are 'S' shaped and laid single-lap began to be imported from Holland at this time, British pantiles, first made at Tilbury in 1701, have the advantage of making a lighter and flatter roof (down to about 30°), so saving on construction costs, and were popular in Somerset and the east and north of Britain. They are often glazed. Machine-made concrete tiles are commonly used today.

Gutters and downpipes When nearly everyone had a thatched house gutters and downpipes were unheard of; the deep thatch absorbed much of the rain and what was left was thrown well clear of the walls by the huge overhang. They first became necessary in towns when stone and tile roofs, both thin and comparatively non-absorbent, became common in the 13th century. The water was discharged through pipes jutting out over the street, saving passers-by from being continually soaked and the decorations painted on the walls from being washed off. Most houses distributed their rainwater evenly around their perimeter which was especially useful in clay areas where it helped to prevent the foundation moving by keeping it damp. Gutters with downpipes were first used to collect water for storage against drought. The materials were generally timber lined with pitch, but lead was used when it could be afforded.

During the latter part of the 16th century lead rainwater-heads and square downpipes began to be used on large houses. The decorative possibilities of moulding the lead were fully exploited with very beautiful results. The fashion continued until the middle of the 18th century when it was finally killed by the classical designers' simpler tastes. Parapets for small houses were first used in towns, where they provided not only a gutter but also protection to pedestrians from falling tiles and snow. They have also provided an unending source of trouble for the householder. Cheap cast iron gutters and downpipes replaced lead during the late 18th century and cheaper plastic is now replacing iron.

1 Castellated parapet on an early l9th century Gothic-style house in Sussex built in brick with finely moulded cement rendering giving the appearance of stone.

2 Half-dormer windows on an early l9th century brick cottage in the Tudor style. Three pointed gables on the front of a house have been popular since Elizabethan times, particularly for farmhouses, with a short intermission during the 18th century. They not only make better use of the roof space but have a dynamic, cheerful aspect. The brick arches over the windows are made from bricks 'rubbed' into segmental shapes centred on the middle of the sill, a technique belonging not to the Tudor period but to the 18th century.

3 Limestone parapet on an early 18th century brick house in Lincoln in the classical style. The local limestone lends itself to fine carving.

4 Reed thatch with a sedge ridge on a roof with three dormer windows on a farm near the Wash.

5 A brick gable with angled courses called 'tumbling' on a cottage in Lincolnshire. This is a common device used in East Anglia particularly Lincolnshire and Norfolk, to save cutting bricks on an exposed weather face. Hand-made bricks are often not so well fired inside as they are on the face. The idea originated with thatched roofs, the brick forming a firm edge to the roofing. The tradition continued long after tiles were introduced – in this area pantiles – which in other areas are used to cover the exposed brick.

6 Late l9th-century house in Hampshire with plain barge boards but decorated ridge tiles. A great deal of Victorian architecture is concerned with breaking up the outline edges of buildings, so nothing is hard and straight: the eye is continuously being waylaid by some new ingenious decoration.

7 A 16th-century lead rainwater-head discharging into the square sectioned pipe used at the time. Rainwater, often a precious commodity collected in butts or underground cisterns, was treated royally in those days and the method of its collection and discharge were considered important formal elements in the design of a house. This example is at Knole, Kent.

Walls

MOST HOUSES HAVE WALLS which are quite distinct from their roofs, but before examining walling methods it should be remembered that there were two ancient methods of house building where the wall and roof were indistinguishable. The first was the early timber triangular house made of branches and covered with sods: a similar system is sometimes used today for small homes using tiles or slates on a timber 'A' frame. The other method was the old stone house where, instead of the roof coming down to the ground, the walls went up and slowly curved in to form a roof. The shape is not unlike a present-day Nissen hut and the structural principle of using one material to perform two different functions is also similar.

Britain was once almost entirely covered in forest so the earliest houses were universally built from timber plugged with mud, sods or stones where these were easily available. It was not until the 14th century, when the great forests had largely been destroyed to make way for agriculture and to be used for fuel and shipbuilding, that ordinary houses began to be built in stone or brick in areas where stone could not be found. Mud was also widely used for the cheapest houses.

Until this time all houses had been remarkably similar, but as soon as builders had to look below the ground for their materials, the great regional variations of material were discovered. This was the start of the long period of nearly four hundred years during which each locality formed its own particular style of building. Some stones, as in the limestone belt, could be cut easily and

so a very refined, delicate style of building emerged. In other areas, such as the granite belts of south-west England, Scotland and Ireland, the stone was too tough to be cut easily and the style of building reflected this quality. In the same way different clays produced regional varieties of colour in brickwork. Those areas where mud and flint naturally occurred and where timber was still plentiful or could easily be imported from Scandinavia (Sussex, Kent and East Anglia) produced further regional differences. The local skills developed in using each of these materials were often much admired by people from other regions. When transport became cheaper in the early 19th century, it was possible to build stone houses in brick areas and vice versa. With increasing competition in the building industry during the 19th century, it was often found cheaper to transport materials a great distance across the country rather than use local stone. The craftsmanship which had been developed to deal with the particular problems posed by local materials has now largely died out – a factor which often makes restoration extremely difficult.

Before carrying out any maintenance to a wall, a careful examination should be made to find any physical defects such as cracks, rising damp and faults in the materials. In old houses it is reassuring to remember that some 'defects', such as slightly bulging walls, flaking brick and stonework, are part of the charm of the building and only need attention if they are structurally dangerous or allow damp penetration. Expert advice should always be sought if there is any doubt. A careful study should be made of

similar houses in the area to find out if any of the same defects occur and how they were dealt with, and also to study the original method of construction; for instance, the original mortar may have been replaced in a previous restoration, but a house near by will show what it should have been.

In timber-frame buildings the worst danger is rot, usually caused by water collecting at a particular point and not being allowed to dry out quickly. This often occurs at joints, the lower ends of vertical members and the top surfaces of horizontal timbers. The most likely place to find rot is in the horizontal sill beam next to the ground where rising damp may have contributed. Fortunately the timber used in old buildings was far stronger than was needed and it is often possible simply to cut away the decayed wood and for appearance sake replace it with a patch of similarly seasoned timber. Sound timber is always 'live' and a timber-frame building is always moving slightly through the seasons. This means that there are always numerous splits and cracks which need to be stopped with an elastic filler. The traditional method was to caulk the joints with hemp and putty. Today it is more efficient to use an appropriate polysulphide mastic (this can be bought in different colours to match the timber work) which, though expensive, is very durable.

There are two basic methods of weatherproofing a timber-frame building. The first is to fill the spaces between the framework, the second is to clad the whole construction right over. The exposed frames have often been considered more decorative and for this reason many timber-framed houses which were

112 ▶

1

2

3

4

5

6

1 Roughly coursed barn wall in Cumbria a mixture of crudely cut granite, basalt and sandstone blocks infilled with split fissile sandstone. At Hesket Newmarket where all these stones are locally available. The slotted opening is framed in brick, once available in the Carlisle area. This is an example of a building that re-uses stone from unwanted structures. Although the barn dates from the late 18th century, some of the stones may have been used in buildings 600 years or more ago.

2 Roughly faced limestone laid dry without mortar. This is the wall of a stone cabin in Co. Clare built in the early 19th century. The holes between the stones were originally packed with clay that has long since washed out. As it is the back of the cabin, the stone has been left its natural colour (the front is limewashed white).

3 A 19th-century dry slate wall in north Wales. The slate has been roughly split into different thicknesses and then sawn across the grain into suitable widths for the wall. This gives a smooth exterior face but random courses. Some unsewn material from an older building has been included, a common practice in rural areas.

4 A mixture of chalk stone and sandstone in a 16th-century cottage wall in Sussex. Both these materials were locally available, the sandstone occurring below the chalk and easily available where the chalk has been eroded. The relative hardnesses of the two materials is quite plain; the chalk was easy to cut to size but has been deeply eroded, the sandstone was rounded by the action of the water in a river-bed but no attempt has been made to cut it to size and it shows no signs of weathering. This wall was originally plastered – the stone was not meant to be exposed.

5 Finely jointed limestone blocks, carefully selected to fit together like pieces of a jigsaw. This is an example of the high quality of craftsmanship available in south-west Ireland in the 11th century.

6 Carefully cut chalk stone in Berkshire laid in irregular courses with fine joints. 113

1

2

3

4

5

6

7

8

9

1 Well weathered Craigleith sandstone (containing a small percentage of lime) in a 17th-century house in Edinburgh. The stone can be cut accurately with a smooth face and has been extensively used for building in Scotland.

2 Finely tooled granite ashlar in southern Ireland in a 19th-century castle. Note the extremely fine joints.

3 A mixture of chalk stone and brick from a house near King's Lynn on the north coast of Norfolk. The bricks are used to help bond the chalk which is in irregular blocks with wide mortared joints.

4 Early 19th-century cottage in Sussex. The walls of the ground floor are in 9 inch cavity brick, laid in economical Chinese bond. The upper floor, shown here, has a timber frame covered in softwood weatherboarding and painted. The combination of these two methods of construction was used for many cottages in the south of England. The brickwork formed a solid rot-proof lower wall and the timberwork above saved paying brick-tax. Sometimes clay tiles were substituted for the weatherboarding.

5 A split flint wall (called 'knapped') with typically wide mortar joints contained between brick vertical and horizontal courses holding the wall together. Part of a l9th-century cottage in the South Downs.

6 Entrance porch of a brick bungalow built in southern England in 1974 faced with thin split Cotswold stone laid in a random pattern.

7 Timber-frame 18th-century house in Surrey covered in decorative clay tiles.

8 18th-century brickwork in a cottage near Reading in Berkshire. The bricks are laid in solid English bond with white lime mortar. This bond is extremely strong. The bricks are hand-made and slightly irregular in colour and shape. The tip of the bricklayer's trowel has been run along the horizontal joints to give an even, delicate appearance, a common practice during the 18th and 19th centuries.

9 Unpainted, finely graded cement rendering on a 19th-century house in London, grooved to simulate ashlar stonework.

originally designed to have their frames covered have their framework exposed. This is easy to spot as the framework itself is always extremely rough and was clearly never expected to be seen. It is well worth restoring such a house to its original appearance after making a careful study of the surrounding buildings. In early buildings close timber frames were filled with laths, square-panel frame houses were filled with wattle work and in both cases clay was applied and finished with a coat of thin plaster. These panels are light and flexible so that they move with the building and any restoration should take this into account. During the 16th century and after, houses were often smartened up by having brickwork inserted which was not only much heavier, leading to distortion of the framework, but also much less flexible, leading to the whole construction being riddled with cracks. Polysulphide mastic joints are the only solution.

One of the great advantages of restoring a timber-frame building entirely covered with tiles, slates or weather-boarding is that these can be fairly easily removed and the framework packed with insulation, so making a far warmer house than before. To keep out draughts the building can be first sheathed in a suitable, permeable building-paper. All battens for attaching tiles or slates should be well treated with preservative and aluminium or copper fixings will save the whole operation having to be re-done for a very long time.

Stone houses fall into two categories: those which use stone simply as a structural material and were rendered, harled or lime-washed over, and secondly those which use stone additionally for its decorative qualities. Since stone is such an expensive material to use, it has often been exposed (like the framing of timber houses which would otherwise have been covered) but this usually means that the house takes on an extremely untidy appearance. Masons naturally took little care in selecting or laying their stones if their work was not to be seen. A further disadvantage is that the wall is liable to become damp, once its protective coating is removed. The sensible solution is to put back a similar rendering to the original.

Stones vary enormously in durability; granite, flint and millstone grit are virtually indestructible and for many houses maintenance can start with a good clean, especially in urban areas. Weaker stone may have

decayed especially if the stone was originally laid incorrectly. In many cases the decay is not serious and rather than risk what are still often experimental treatments it is better to leave it. In very bad cases expert help should be sought but only from the best authorities – many buildings have been ruined by inexpert treatment. Frequently stone buildings have been damaged by the iron cramps used to bind the stones together or by iron window bars and railings. The iron corrodes and splits stonework. The best solution is to replace the embedded iron with rustless metal. Great care should be taken in choosing the right mortar for repointing. This can often be established by examining the old mortar in similar buildings near by, which will usually be found to be either white or a similar colour to the stone. Any new stonework should be carried out in exactly the same manner as the original. Very good results were achieved in a remote part of Somerset by using a one-eyed mason after he had had his midday cider. The walls he built were indistinguishable from the original.

The main difference between stone and brickwork is that, except for the harder stones, brick lasts better. Only under-fired or badly made bricks decay, and when this happens it usually affects only one or two bricks in a wall. They can either be left as part of the patina of age, since they rarely affect the structural stability, or be simply cut out and replaced with similar bricks, if they can be found, perhaps cut out from a less important part of the house. Additional brickwork should match the original as closely as possible if the house is to remain homogeneous in appearance. With old brickwork mortar should be white, like old lime mortar, so the full character and colour of the bricks are shown. The actual mortar joint should be copied from the old pattern of which there are a great many varieties; the most efficient is flush pointing. Many walls were either built too thin or of bricks which were too porous and have had a waterproof rendering applied. If the bricks were decorative, it is worth considering removing the rendering and treating the wall with a transparent waterproofer.

Mud walls are difficult to repair. If they were made of clay bats, it is possible to cut out individual blocks and replace them with new. Regular mud walls can only be repaired by cutting out a complete section of a wall and re-building, using a similar technique as in the past.

Doors and windows

THE MOST IMPORTANT outside feature of a house is the front door: in early houses it was usually the only one. The door served not only as a gangway for men and animals, it was often the only source of light. To keep the draught out, an ox hide or coarse fabric was used that could be pulled up like a blind, a custom which persisted in the north of Scotland until the 18th century (the bead curtain still found on the Continent is a descendant of the same principle). The first solid doors were stone slabs, but as skills were developed wattle and timber doors were introduced as better and lighter alternatives. The early timber doors were made from a series of solid planks, fixed together with cross planks on the back in the same way as a ledged shed door is made today. Superior doors were made with vertical and horizontal planks spiked together with wood or metal nails. There were no door frames, the door was simply hung by metal straps on to metal pins driven into the stone or timber frame of the house. Many of these doors can still be found.

It is difficult to make a door close neatly on to the structure of a house, and during the 16th century door frames were introduced. The advent of the door frame, so much more accurate in shape, made it possible to abandon the old pin hinges and to use flat hinges instead. Early hinges consisted of long vertical iron strips fixed to the face of the frame, connected to long horizontal strips fixed to one or both sides of the door. They had to be very strong to support the weight of the solid doors and were marvellous examples of the blacksmith's art, often shaped into clever patterns. As the skill of

the carpenters and joiners improved in the 17th century, these heavy doors were replaced by the framed and panelled door, which was much lighter and used far less timber. This made it possible to use 'H' hinges which had vertical straps on the door as well as on the frame, thus missing the panels. During the 18th century the cast iron butt was introduced, fixed to the inside faces of the frame and door, as today, and almost completely concealed.

For most of its history the timber front door has been solid: it was either open to let in the light and visitors or it was closed against the stranger and the weather. During the late 19th century front doors began to have their upper panels replaced with glass, always obscured and often coloured.

The concealed mortice lock did not arrive until the 19th century. Door knockers and pull handles were introduced during the 18th century – normally of painted cast iron. Only a few could afford brass and yet in much restoration work it seems that most people cannot resist using it, despite all the bother of cleaning. The lazy can be reassured that cast iron is usually more correct.

Letter boxes were not introduced until the 19th century and on an old door they often destroy the symmetry. Either paint them so that they do not show or put them in a side panel. In every case it is essential to use door fittings which suit the design of the door and fortunately it is not difficult to find second-hand or reproduction fittings. For a special case it is reasonably cheap to have them made to order if a prototype can be borrowed. ▶

1   Typical half-door on a small cabin outside Cashel in Co. Tipperary in Eire. The advantage of the half-door is that you can open and lean on it while keeping chickens and other animals out.

2   Plain door on a 19th-century cottage in Sussex. The letterbox is an addition.

3   5ft 6 in. (1675 mm) door in a 17th-century cottage at Ennis, Co. Clare, Eire. Cottage doors of this period and earlier are often very low demonstrating the shortness of people in those times.

4   Late 18th-century door on a house in Cumbria.

5   Early 18th-century door on a house in Cumbria.

6   Early 19th-century door on a house in Cumbria.

7   Late 18th-century door in Aberaeron, Dyfed, Wales.

8   Doorway in Bedford Square, London, built in 1775 with artificial (Coade) stone.

9   Late 18th-century farmhouse in Berkshire with a 19th-century trellis porch.

10   Door and porch on a 19th-century cottage at Calne, Wiltshire.

11   Early 19th-century door with cast iron decoration in Bayswater, London.

12   Arabian-style cast-iron porch and balcony on a late 19th-century house in King's Lynn, Norfolk.

1

2

3

4

5

6

7

8

9

10

11

12

Windows The word window came from 'wind-hole' – an opening in the wall or roof to let in air for the fire, facing away from the prevailing wind. If light were needed the door was left open; hence the phrase 'never darken my doorway again'. To stop birds and other intruders, the wind-hole was often criss-crossed in a diamond pattern with reeds or wickerwork, the sloping design shedding the rainwater away. This design was later copied for lead lights and is still used today. A more substantial method was to place vertical bars of squared oak, set at an angle so that they reflected light into the room and placed 3 to 6 in. (75 x 150 mm) apart. The simplest way of keeping the weather out was to use a sliding or hinged shutter. In stone houses which had thick walls, the sides of the wind-hole openings were often sloped back to give better lighting inside, while in timber-framed houses the wind-hole was simply a gap left between timber. Since wind-holes were a source of draughts and damp, they were kept to a minimum and many small houses had none at all.

Although the Romans made glass at Glastonbury and had perfected methods of rolling out quite large slabs of sheet glass for windows, these techniques were not used after they left. Any glass Britain needed was imported, and the Normans brought it at high cost from France, Flanders and Germany for use in churches and large houses that could afford weatherproof windows. The glass came in small pieces in varying thicknesses and was joined together by narrow cast-lead cames. These windows were fixed on iron frames and hung on hooks so they were easily removable. They were expensive and small, were placed high up out of reach of possible thieves and, being treated as furnishings, were removed from house to house with the owner until a law banned this in 1579. However, by then glass had become much cheaper with the development of the home glass industry which had started after 1200 in a small way in Surrey, Staffordshire, Shropshire and Cheshire, where suitable sands were available. Although large houses had been using glass throughout the 16th century, it was only after 1600 that the ordinary man could afford it; indeed, parts of Ireland, Wales and Scotland had to wait until the early 19th century. Until then a variety of methods had been used to provide cheap substitutes, for example, oiled fabric or paper and the afterbirth of cattle, an idea possibly introduced by the Norse; the Irish preferred that of a mare, as it was said

to be bayonet proof. Other alternatives, thin horn, alabaster or mica, were almost as expensive as glass. 17th-century glass was still blown as a disc and only available in small pieces, none larger than about 10 in. (254 mm) in length. Cast-lead cames gave way to cheaper milled cames, often with beaded edges, and by the 18thcentury they were extremely thin and elegant and the dark holes became elegantly fretted spaces. From the design point of view, windows had been considered as dark spaces in solid walls, but a great revolution came in the late 17th century with the introduction from Holland of the vertical sliding sash window made in wood. No leaded window could stand the stresses of being pushed up and down, so white-painted timber replaced lead. Wood windows were considered a great fire hazard, however, and a law was passed in 1709 requiring all timber frames to be set back from the wall face. Most early sashes were fixed at the top and only the lower sash could be pushed up and then held in place by a hook. By the end of the 18th century the counterbalanced double-sash replaced this system, the bars had become exceedingly thin, and the whole window was as structurally interdependent as a modern aircraft. These vertical sashes had to be tall. For smaller squared windows, the horizontal sliding window was invented early in the 18th century by a Yorkshireman. Casement windows were still preferred for stone houses, but the sash reigned supreme in all brick and timber-clad buildings. During the 19th century durable cast-iron casements often replaced wood, especially in cottages. Between 1696 and 1851 various taxes based on the number of windows in a house caused many old houses to have windows blocked up and limited their use generally.

In the 20th century the steel casement window replaced the older complicated timber sash. New timber casements were also produced to compete with steel. After the 1939 war aluminium sliding windows or even frameless windows in thick plate glass were introduced. Georgian-style windows and leaded lights are still with us, but in both cases the divisions are too fat and clumsy for true restoration work. Many otherwise beautiful houses have been ruined because their leaded lights were changed to Georgian or their Georgian sashes were replaced with Victorian sheet glass or by modern picture windows. Windows are the eyes of a house; change them and the whole character is lost.

1 16th-century leaded lights in a timber frame house in Cheshire. The decorative patterns of lead cames disguise the fact that large pieces of glass were difficult and expensive to make at that time.

2 19th-century Gothic Revival cast-iron casement window in a cottage in Hertfordshire. Many very decorative windows of this type were produced in standard sizes at this time and were widely used for cottages.

3 18th-century leaded casement window in a thatched cottage in Bedfordshire.

4 Typical Scottish dormer window with angled sides to see down the street on a single-storey cottage in Tayside.

5 Late 18th-century sash window with Gothic Revival top in south west Eire. Round-headed windows are often found in classical houses, especially single detached ones, generally to light a landing or staircase.

6 Early 19th-century Gothic Revival window in Cashel, Tipperary, Eire.

7 Early 19th-century Gothic Revival window in East Marston, Yorkshire.

8 Early 19th-century Gothic Revival window in Surrey. The top of the window is a flattened ogee shape, a popular form of arch in the 16th century when it was borrowed from early Italian Gothic. Reintroduced in the late 18th century, it was much used during the 19th.

9 19th-century casement window in a cottage at Bishop's Nympton, near Barnstaple in Devonshire.

10 Early 19th-century sliding sash window in Sussex. Sliding windows are often thought to be a modern innovation, but they were commonly used during the 18th and early 19th centuries, especially for rural buildings. With low ceilings and squat windows, horizontally sliding sashes were a practical and cheap solution.

11 Simple late 19th-century sash window in Ballyvaughan, Co. Clare, Eire.

12 A typical 1910 semi-detached house with a projecting oriel window over the front door and a rounded bay. The windows follow the Tudor style but only the upper lights are leaded; the lower ones are in single sheets of glass for better vision and light.

1

2

3

4

5

6

7

8

9

10

11

12

Paving, paths and boundaries

PUTTING DOWN PAVING OUTSIDE is like taking a carpet into the garden: it is something which essentially belongs to the house, an extension of the floor inside. Just as in interior decoration, the type of paving must be chosen to match the surroundings. Another way of considering paving is to liken it to the roots of a tree, the trunk being the house; paving attaches a house to its surroundings. In the past local stones, cobbles, pebbles (often placed in decorative patterns dating back to neolithic times) or gravel were used. From the 14th-century bricks and brick tiles could also be obtained. An architectural ideal of the classical period was to build and pave, both inside and out, in the same material, usually stone, with visually grand results. The same degree of homogeneity on a simpler scale is achieved in many stone areas such as Wales, where slate is used for the walls of the house and for all the paving and flooring. In Sussex and Kent many villages and houses have brick paving matching the brick or tile hung houses.

Today, with the vast choice of paving available, it is easy to fall into the trap of putting neat flat paving against an old wall so that each shows the defects of the other. Old paving should always be cherished and re-used (as it often already has been) wherever possible, and new paving chosen and laid only after a careful study of local methods. Brick paving laid on compact earth or sand will naturally form a slightly uneven surface and will look much better against an old brick house than one laid on a concrete base in order to be regular, level and weed-free. Conversely, an old-style irregular stone paving will look equally odd against a new paving will look equally odd against a new

wall. In planning new paving, two things must be remembered: the first is that paths must be in the most convenient place if they are to be used – laziness is endemic. The second is that, once away from the immediate area of the house, the lines of paths can be freer and a gentle curve (remember the eye will see a much sharper curve walking along the path than is seen on plan) might give a much more natural and inviting entrance to, say, a Victorian cottage – like the roots of a tree. This is not a rule for every house; straight paths and paving are usually needed for classical designs.

As paths point out the way, so boundary walls define ownership. They can also be used as protection against wind or traffic noise, to provide privacy or a warm wall to sit against long after the sun has gone down. Hedges can be a haven for birds and small animals and a source of fruit and decorations for the flower vase. Walls can also support small flowers, creepers and lichens, as well as trained fruit trees. Like paths, walls are an extension of the house and must be treated with the same care. A walled garden is like an outside room.

Each locality has its own traditional walling system ranging from the thatched mud walls of Devon to the rows of split-limestone slabs, like so many tombstones, of Caithness. Hedges, more or less penetrable, can be clipped to imitate walls (when they take up little room), but this means that they should be of one kind: yew, beech, privet or similar. Ideally the choice depends on the date of the house. Where there is more space, the hedge can be mixed: blackberry, thorn, ash, willow, dog rose, beech, hazel, trav-

1 Simple 19th-century wrought iron railings and gate at Avebury, Wiltshire.

2 Chalk stone paving in Sussex.

3 Pebble paving in Kent.

4 Section through a dry-stone wall in Cumbria.

5 Victorian gate in Wales.

6 Stone and turf wall in Knockananna, Co. Limerick, Eire.

7 Sandstone wall in Cumbria.

8, 9 Variations in pebble paving, Aberystwyth, Dyfed, Wales.

10 Loose stone paving in Cumbria.

11 Brick paving in Sussex.

ellers' joy, holly, hornbeam, to give a variety of different delights throughout the year. The hedge is then part of the garden and not of the house. Iron fences such as the standard park fence present little visual barrier but their straight lines link them to the house. Timber fences of the post-and-rail type common in the south of England need space to look their best. Wood picket fences, especially when painted white (they were popular in the 19th century), are useful for small gardens, but the solid creosoted board fence is a poor substitute for a wall. The most invisible fence is a ha-ha; a ditch too wide for animals to jump, it is also useful for drainage.

1

2

3

4

5

6

7

8

9

10

11

Conservatories, garages and other extensions

ONE OF THE MOST CONTROVERSIAL PARTS of a house is the design of the outbuildings or extension. How it relates to the whole composition should show not only the history of the building but also how the inhabitants wish to present themselves to the outside world. Sometimes they are part of the original design and layout of the design. Perhaps, now, their use has changed with changes in technology and the function for which they were intended have become obsolete or newer ways of living mean that previously unknown manners have occupied them. Separate privies and even piggeries are now converted for extended domestic habitation. The three types of outbuilding can be described with the first being the accommodation of animals, transport and other agricultural equipment. These are the most common and can be found in the earliest dwellings recorded. The second is the addition of space for nurturing exotic plants in a well tempered environment, these date from the 16th century in the larger houses reaching the smaller town houses by the middle of the nineteenth century. Last the extension for providing washing facilities within the house are comparatively recent when one considers that the first building in Europe to be fully serviced was Pentonville Prison built in 1840.

The animals in the earliest settled homes were kept on the ground floor of the house with humans sleeping alongside or better above on racks forming an upper storey so benefiting from the warmth of the animals. Later a separate entrance would be made for the animals, this was the first separation followed by the cowshed or stable becoming a separate, attached building. The stables would have had accommodation for the groom sleeping above the horses in the grander houses, for reasons of both security and economy. The mews house in towns is such a building type . The last farm in which animals and humans slept under the same roof was still being used in such way in Sussex until the early nineteen seventies. In towns and cities the stabling of horses and coaches would occupy quite some considerable amount of space until the arrival of the motorcar which could be left out in the street, so freeing up stabling for domestic use.

The first garages for the motorised carriage often in their design included a room for the chauffeur above with a room for a workshop. The post First World War suburban house developments when they included a garage would have it separate from the house as a distinct building, designed in harmony with the main house. These would be just large enough to accommodate a small family car or motorcycle combination of the period within a space of 10 x 7 ft (3 x 2.1 m). Windows are minimal and the door is designed in an utilitarian version of the house style.

The doors of the stable were designed for the passage of animals and carriages, often with a smaller human sized door set within the larger. Made of solid timber and hung on iron straps, they were intended to be handled and touched. The modern 'up and over' garage door is by contrast only touched at its car - boot - like handle or not at all when operated by remote sensor. These can often have the pristine appearance of a giant fridge door next to the house. ▶

1   A pair of late-18th-century timber houses, one of which has replaced its original windows for plastic ill-proportioned insertions that destroy the harmony of the facade. Properly constructed timber sash windows without the 'ears' below the top sash which is correct for a house built before 1865 can be made surprisingly inexpensively bought.

2   A seaside house in Dorset that started its life as a second-class railway carriage. It has since been clad in fake stonework to match its neighbours. This has lost to the public the true face of its particular history.

3   A large double car garage built as an integral part of the relatively small new house. The structure is timber frame with a brick skin and panels of precast flints applied to maintain a variety of local vernacular design in this 1990s development in Sussex.

4   A modern vernacular house built using modern structural construction techniques but clad in familiar materials to create a false impression. Designed with an integral garage specifically to follow planning guidelines that stipulate the number of car spaces per household to keep cars off the road. The integral garage has now been appropriated for domestic use and the car is now left outside again.

5   The architect J.C. Loudon's experiment with curvilinear forms in glazing is shown in a conservatory of 1818 placed proudly on the front of his own London house. The curved wrought-iron glazing bars were an invention of his, thus making it possible to produce this form. It complements the Classical Greek revival architecture of the main contemporary house in a way that the pitched roof of a conventional structure could never achieve.

1

2

3

4

5

123

The incorporation of the garage back into the house is a late twentieth century demand that planning has contrived. With increased reliance on the car as a means to live and get to work the front garden is now given over to the vehicle if space is lacking to the side. Contemporary photographs of modern houses of the 1920s would often place a car in front of the house reinforcing the connection of the architecture to the time. American influenced driveways are not just after-thoughts as somewhere to get the car off the street but pedestals on which to place the car, like a statue, in a composition on the drive-way in front of the house. The modern ver-nacular house often has the ground floor given over to the garaging of cars. Once again, the ground floor is used as accommo-dation for transport which completes a cycle back to the primitive farmstead or mews house.

Since garages usually face the road, under-standing how one reads the front of a house is very important, the rule being that the main house should be clearly seen as the dominant element. The way of demonstrat-ing the hierarchy of human to animal to plant to vehicle is clearly shown in the better designs. Confusing entrances can destroy the harmony of a house. Panelling of garage doors should match the balance of the house and be plainer; fancy cornices around garage extensions that are intended to 'tie the build-ing in' only serve to confuse the eye and diminish the sense of hierarchy that all the best buildings have. Paint is a way of har-monising the two structures whilst allowing them to retain their separate identities.

The backs and sides of houses tend to be traditionally where all the messy pipes and services were put and it is only comparative-ly recently that the smaller house has had to consider its rear elevation. The conservatory, by contrast with the garage, often has the task of trying to improve this aspect of the older house. Traditionally the greenhouse for growing food was strictly utilitarian with simple unadorned structures of sensible pro-portions that were for the express purpose of raising edible plants. The conservatory, as we now know it, is a rediscovery of a particu-lar building type that developed in the nineteenth century as an extension to the home and was ignored for the first half of the twentieth century.

The glass house as first introduced to England by Sir Thomas Gresham in the 16th-century, was a place to nurture the prized orange tree and other citrus plants. This was the preserve of the larger house enabling the owner to collect exotic plants in a controlled environment. The orangery is distinct from the glasshouse or conservatory in that a solid roofed construction was used with large windows as the plants are only housed in the heated orangery during the winter; in the summer the plants would be moved outside in their pots the building could be given over to indoor games and garden dinners.

Glass roofs for greenhouses and conserva-tories began first to appear at the beginning of the nineteenth century to create a climate suitable for the tropical plants, now arriving from all corners of the Empire, that had to be housed all year round. Since glass was taxed on pane size and quality, the pieces of glass used tended to be small and thicker than house glass. A greenish colour tinge and a mottled appearance still appears in the 'hor-ticultural glass' available today at a much lower price than plate glass. This glass, inci-dentally, is also good for restoring the effect of old spun glass in Georgian houses.

The conservatory was attached to the house as a place for displaying plants from an unfolding world to admiring visitors. Gardeners were employed to constantly monitor these carefully maintained environ-ments. Cast iron was the new material that made possible the slender supports of these structures distinguishing them from the util-itarian greenhouse in the kitchen garden. Strength, thinness and proportion are the qualities of cast and wrought iron sections over timber and this was fully exploited in the curvilinear designs of J.C. Loudon and others which break away from the rectilinear box with a pitched roof. New approaches to glass for conservatories in the twentieth cen-tury started with the unique Witley Park underwater 'crystal cavern' made from glass four inches thick.

Prefabrication of cast iron, a material that uses decoration as a disguise for the defects of casting, made possible a new form of architecture; transparent, curving winter palaces for palm trees and other exotic won-ders. The advantage of cast iron is that, as it cools, it expands slightly before continuing to shrink. This takes up all the detail in the mould and so makes possible the mass pro-duction of details that would previously have had to be carved. The modern replace-ment, aluminium, on the other hand, just shrinks at a steady rate and so loses the finer details and comes out looking heavily over-painted in form. In keeping with the time, the references were the finials and floral ▶

6 A row of seaside cabins which demon-strate architecturally what the relationship between a room and the sun is. The veran-dah in miniature and as such a reminder of the aspiration that a conservatory aims for if the plants are not important.

7 Even though these small 1960s timber clad houses have purpose-built integral garages, one suspects that, as in the stable before, the now larger car has been forced out onto the drive.

8 A small summer-house built in timber and based on an 18th-century Gothick fire-place design sits in a London garden as a perfect example of a correctly proportioned modern folly fulfilling all the needs of a gar-den room.

9 A small detached stone early-19th-cen-tury stable just outside Dublin that clearly shows its purpose and function with a witty flourish. The restrained detailing on the rest of the building gives it a dignity rather than a pedestrian quality. An example of how a clear design thought can work with any material.

10 An honest 19th-century greenhouse that does not upstage the building behind by being free of the application of pretentious ornament. Simply proportioned and spa-cious. Originally it was complemented by a more ornate conservatory in the adjacent garden, but it is worth noting the benefits of this traditional structure.

11 A large embellished conservatory occu-pying the courtyard of an early 18th-century house. It has taken over the role of the front door, which now faces a busy road, and so disguises the true nature of the house with its florid railway station style of construc-tion. A slightly clumsy composition but typi-cal of the type of conservatory that is cur-rently in vogue.

12 A typical late-20th-century suburban-sprawl house that appears to be a chance meeting between its various elements. Porch, garage and main house all fight for attention and one is still not really sure where the main entrance is.

13 A simple lean-to glasshouse on a mid-19th-century town house that boasts a veran-dah. The thin bars and lack of decoration mean that the glass can appear like a stretched fabric beside the substantially built house.

6

7

8

9

10

11

12

13

flourishes of the Greek and Gothick revivals and, using the technique of casting iron – so becoming a first use of prefabrication in British houses – spread from the landed gentry to the affluent middle classes. Serviced by gardeners they lasted until the First World War.

During the latter part of the 20th-century the conservatory became an extra room to the house, taking the house into the garden rather than exotic plants into the house. Now conservatories are the modern sitting room or garden room with people enjoying the advantage they bring of light and sun in a temperature-controlled environment. They might contain a swimming pool rather than a collection of plants. Visually this means that the white glazing bars are not set off by a mass of dark green foliage but by the furnishings of leisure.

Appropriate styles for conservatories need to work with the history of the house they are being fitted to. The domestic conservatory, being a 19th-century invention, is still being made mimicking an ornate style of finials and ridge decoration, rather like provincial railway architecture. This may be appropriate on a house built between say 1840 and 1914 but is not appropriate with anything built after this date and looks fussy and clumsy when attached to anything earlier. A Victorian design looks ridiculous tacked onto an Exmoor longhouse since it is being dishonest to both traditions. Conservatory manufacturers now provide a range of styles using aluminium and UPVC instead of cast iron and incorporating double or triple glazing with thermal breaks and other improved environment controls. They range from the simple to the sophisticated but there is still a muddled sense of history, to the extent that louvred cupolas from stables are now appearing on conservatories to satisfy an environmental concern in a confused nostalgia mixing the garage with the greenhouse. If one remembers the recommendations of creating a suitable 'history' for the house then a 1940s neoclassical design of a simple galvanised steel structure is perhaps more appropriate on a Georgian house than the proportions of 19th-century Greek revival.

The recent development of completely glass structures for conservatories uses structural glass beams made of tempered and laminated glass for support instead of timber or aluminium. These make a minimal modern solution to the problem of extending a house that would otherwise become visually confused and lose its dominance if a fussy conservatory with thick white glazing bars

14

were spliced on. Structural glass conservatories are almost completely transparent structures and when used to the rear of an older house minimise the visual impact. When used sensitively the conservatory can provide a far more fitting solution than the standard Victorian structure and in certain situations can be adapted to classical proportions. The structural glass conservatory can be made with triple glazing and incorporate all the environmental controls such as blinds and vents to meet all modern domestic requirements.

Sensitive use of colour with a thin section of glazing bar with sympathetically proportioned glazing sections can help considerably in the matching of the styles. Darker colours will tend to disappear against a brick house, so making the design more discreet. Glazing bars in Georgian houses were often painted in black or dark Brunswick green to reduce the visual impact of the windows. White was used in the Victorian conservatory to make it stand out as a symbol of prestige set visually from the rest of the house like a jewelled reliquary containing a collection of exotic examples collected by the owner.

Nowadays we have to be just as clear as to what an addition is saying on an older build-

ing. The simple social codes of our ancestors for an extension, such as sergeants' and corporals' 'stripes', derive from the size of their home. The primitive 'A frame' cruck house required two inverted timber Vs to form a shelter. Upon promotion the householder would be awarded an extra cruck which would be added to form a two-bay dwelling. This is why, to this day, one does not see the single inverted V emblazoned on the uniform of the British army private because it is impossible to build a building with only one cruck.

14 A simple timber conservatory that respects the lines of the existing building and by using a bold proportion of timber does not appear to be a converted greenhouse. The house is sympathetically let into the garden and has had its privies and ramshackle outbuildings tidied away in the process.

15 The first conservatory in the world using structural glass, designed by the architect Rick Mather with the engineer Tim Macfarlane in 1990. The building technique uses sophisticated glues and sealants and can be triple-glazed with the most modern environmental controls.

Protective treatments

FIRST STUDY THE DESIGN of the house to see if any improvements should be made: an unsightly porch removed, window bars put back or a television aerial put in a better position. If the house is of any age, check with the local planning office to see if it is scheduled as a building of architectural interest or in a conservation area. If it is, it may be possible to get a grant towards the work. Next, check the house for structural defects. Chimneys are often neglected, but even recent houses can have stacks badly damaged by the combined effects of sulphuric acid from smoke and moisture from the combustion gases which eat away the mortar joints. Stacks should be carefully repointed using a suitable mortar mix of cement:lime:sand of appropriate colour. If the flue is no longer used it should be capped with a flat slate with a small hole in the centre, making sure there is free ventilation from below. Lead flashings to chimney stacks are a 19th-century innovation: older houses had simple mortar flaunching. Both these if they deteriorate will cause damp. The roof should be examined and any defects remedied.

Gutters and drainpipes are a common cause of damp penetration. They should be checked to make sure that all joints are sound, that the gutters have the right fall and that they are clear of debris. Where downpipes discharge over an open gully this should be cleaned out. Both these jobs should be done at least once a year.

Parapets and copings are another frequent source of damp: the pointing and gutter behind should be carefully examined. The most frequent problem with copings is water penetration through the joints. Ideally they should be lifted and bedded on a damp-proof course. Alternatively, the coping stone joints can be sealed with glass fibre and Bitumen Basecoat followed by treatment with exterior mineral paint using a colour to match the original stone. Many Victorian houses have heavy mouldings on the face and sometimes these have either fallen off or been removed. As a result the facade will have lost its character and in these circumstances it is well worth considering replacement. There is usually at least one house nearby still complete enough from which a pattern can be taken. This job is one for a skilled plasterer but it will greatly improve the appearance and value of the house.

Timber walls should be carefully examined for signs of rot, likely to occur in places where rain-water can be trapped: the foot of verticals, the top of horizontals, joints in the framing. Any decayed wood should be cut out and replaced and the surrounding timber well treated with preservative. Timber buildings are always moving, so joints should be filled with mastic (preferably a polysulphide of appropriate colour) never with a hard-setting material. Damaged weather-boarding should be replaced with boards cut to the same pattern as the original. This costs little extra, but vastly improves the visual effect. Early weather-boarding usually has a groove along the bottom edge. Old exposed framework, which should have been left to weather naturally, was often painted black with tar during the last century. The tar can be cleaned off with strong caustic soda, handled with great care, the timber should then be lime washed, left for a few days and finally wire brushed down. If the walls are of stone or brick they may need re-pointing. The joints should be raked out for $1/2$ in. (12 mm) and then pointed up with an appropriate cement:lime:sand mortar to match the original. If there is any doubt, flush pointing is the most efficient. Old houses should have white cement in the mortar to simulate the original white lime. However, if colour pointing is needed a coloured cement can be used. In urban areas the stone- or brickwork may need a good clean, but if the stone is at all weak or decayed use the best expert advice before doing anything. Many fine stone buildings have been ruined for ever by inexpert cleaning: it would have been far better to have left them as they were. Some times an odd stone has been laid incorrectly (stones should be laid in the same way as they were originally deposited), or an under-fired brick or two may have decayed. It is possible to patch the wall. Usually there is no structural problem: they can be left as part of the mellowing of time. Structural defects such as cracks or bulges need expert professional advice. Often these are caused by slight subsidence which has since stopped. Others may be due to more continuing subsidence, the thrust from a roof truss or rotting timbers originally incorporated in the wall to strengthen it. Renderings are applied for various reasons. They are either there to water-proof a wall as in the case of many timber-framed houses, or to disguise a poorer facing material, as in the case of Regency stucco or the pebble-dash of between-the-wars housing. If you do decide ▶

128

Pebble dash
Like all rough sufaces is difficult to clean. Best treatment for old unpainted pebble dash is the Snowcem/Sandtex Matt system.

Guttering
Guttering and downpipes which are faulty are a prime cause of damp. Clear gutters of debris, make all joints water-tight and check fall.

Flaunching
Cracked flaunching can be a cause of damp around chimney pots and elsewhere on older houses. Repair with mortar to match.

Sills
Bare timber sills and thresholds need oiling. Drip grooves under sills must be cleared out to be effective. Cracked stone sills can be repaired and painted.

Roofing
should be examined and defects remedied. Use secondhand tiles/slates to match existing roof. Stone and thatch need expert attention.

Parapets
and copings are a frequent source of damp. The joints, flashing and gutter behind should be checked and repaired where necessary.

Timber framing
Examine for signs of rot where water may be trapped. Joints can be filled with a non-setting mastic which lets the timbers move.

Windows
Timber windows should be checked for wet rot and any defective sections replaced. Metal windows should be checked for rust.

Chimneys
Sulphuric acid from smoke and damp eat away mortar. If poor, rebuild or repair if necessary. Seal unused flues with a ventilated slate.

Flashings
Lead flashings can crack and cause damp penetration. Pointing and flashing should be checked and replaced to effect a cure.

Rendering
Large cracks in smooth rendering can be filled using Bitumen Basecoat/Sandtex matt system with glass fibre.

Cladding
Split or rotting timber cladding should be replaced with matching sections and treated with a timber preservative – not varnished – and painted if necessary.

Tile hung walls
Broken tiles should be replaced with matching secondhand tiles. (Ivy and other climbers can lift tiles away from the battens causing cracks.)

Friable or dusty wall surfaces
Before decoration remove loose material and treat with Blue Circle Stabilising Solution.

amp penetration
ough solid wall nstruction ot rising damp which ould be seen to parately): treat ole area or building th Blue Circle Bitumen secoat followed by ndtex.

Gulleys
Rainwater downpipes ideally discharge into an open gulley and this should be thoroughly cleaned out at regular intervals.

Damp proofing
Broken or non-existent damp-proof courses can cause rising damp. Specialist firms should be asked to advise on cures.

Brickwork
may need repointing. Rake out joints, repoint in 1:2:8 mortar mix coloured to match. Use white cement in mix to match old lime mortar.

Stonework
If stonework is weak or decayed, get expert advice before cleaning. Replace worn stonework with matching material. Repoint as for brick.

Air bricks
Blocked air bricks stop underfloor ventilation and this causes dry rot in floor timbers. Keep earth and plants away from air bricks.

Wood and metal
New timber: prime undercoat and finish gloss. Old timber: rub down, undercoat and finish in gloss. Rust spots on metal: treat with rust inhibitor undercoat and finish gloss.

to strip off deteriorated rendering and replace it always bring it back to its original appearance. Any grooves in smooth rendering simulating stonework should carefully be mapped out and reproduced.

Most solid walls can be waterproofed by the application of bitumen basecoat followed by matt masonry paint, the exception being walls where natural appearance is important such as those made of stone. Treatment with exterior waterproofer which is clear, may be used in such cases. Movement cracks can be treated by first filling them with cement and sand and treating with bitumen basecoat and glass fibre (to the manufacturer's recommendation) followed by a fine textured resin-based masonry paint finish. Very fine hair cracks can be filled with a mixture of masonry paint and Portland cement worked well in. After filling wipe over with a damp sponge to remove any surplus from the face of the rendering and ensure that everything has dried out before applying any decoration.

Most smooth renderings, or stucco, were intended to be decorated. Until the introduction of oil paint in the 19th century, water-based paints were used, the intention being to give the impression of stonework as far as possible. The glossy cream oil paint now associated with Regency is far from the original appearance. If the house is part of a terrace, already gloss painted, it is probably best to continue using the same paint. If the house is on its own, then it can be restored to something like its original appearance by using a fine-textured masonry paint.

Some rough renderings, like the traditional Scottish harling, were lime-washed, but the modern alternative, Tyrolean finish, is self-coloured. Dry dash, the most common rendering used this century, depends on the colour of the stones, pebble, burnt flints or even sea shells, thrown onto it for its decorative effect. Unfortunately none of these rough surfaces is easy to clean and the best solution, especially if it has had to be patched, is to use a mineral painted method of decoration.

There are three enemies to lasting decoration: and perhaps the most damaging is damp, particularly that from behind which pushes off the paint surface. Many houses have either a defective damp-proof course or none at all so that damp rises directly from the ground into the wall. There are a number of specialist firms who can deal with this. Something anyone can do is to check that the damp-proof course is 150mm

(6 in.) above the ground, and that the rendering is no lower, causing a bridge for damp. Any adjacent paving should slope to drain away from the wall. Brown soot stains can penetrate the outside decoration of damp chimneys, which should be given impervious linings and the stains painted over with leafing grade aluminium paint before final decoration.

Damp in a different form on the surface caused perhaps by overhanging trees or a north aspect will allow algal growth. It is essential that organic growth be treated with a suitable fungicide otherwise the algal growth will recur under the new decoration causing it to fail. All surfaces to be decorated must be sound. Any loose material must be removed and weak and dusty surfaces can be treated with stabilising solution after thorough cleaning down.

Iron and other metalwork (gutters, downpipes, railings, door furniture) needs close examination and thorough cleaning down. Rusty areas should be carefully wire-brushed and then treated with a rust inhibitor, followed by an appropriate paint. Open joints and cracks should be filled with red or white lead putty. Bare spots in galvanising should be touched in with zinc or calcium plumbate primer after cleaning. The insides of metal gutters should be painted with two coats of bituminous paint.

Timber windows and doors should be carefully checked for rot and any defective sections replaced. The drip grooves under sills and opening windows and doors should be cleaned out so that they are effective. Make sure that the vulnerable top edges are painted, often they are not because they are out of sight. Bare timber sills and thresholds need to be liberally oiled.

There is an enormous number of paints on the market for painting metal and woodwork. In making your choice, remember that in all painting the value of the work far exceeds the cost of the materials: it pays to buy the best.

Despite the care that may be taken in deciding and specifying the work to be done, the final quality of the job rests with the individual carrying it out and his supervision. The cheapest job is often the least economic in the long run: all too usually it means that the estimate has not taken fully into account the difficulties to be encountered. But to be really sure, there is nothing like doing it yourself – with appropriate advice.

1 This terrace of early 19th-century houses, designed in the Greek classical style, depends on fine proportion and detailing for its effect. During their history a number of soil pipes, vents and telephone cables are often added without regard to the original design of houses. Wires can be rerouted along mouldings at little or no extra cost and pipework run inside (where it is less likely to freeze up and saves maintenance). If this is too expensive, the pipes can be painted to match the wall behind, as in this example.

2 A terrace of small Georgian cottages depending on the unity of the group for their effect. The roofs were originally all slate, renovation has led to a variety of different materials being used, so destroying the visual harmony of the group.

3 Paint is often associated with newness and smartness, both quite inappropriate for this pair of 17th-century cottages where the original clay wall tiles have been ruined for ever.

4 This pair of sedate late 19th-century houses once had a pleasant regularity of design, now lost through the conversion of one-half to the lightweight style of the 1960s.

5 This pair of late 19th-century houses once had the same front doors, now one is all glass, as if one stocking had fallen.

6 Both the visual and actual value of this pair of early 19th-century cottages has been lost by converting one to the style of the 1950s. The excellent brickwork has been rendered, the carefully proportioned, expensive timber windows replaced with much cheaper standard steel and the openings altered to fit. It is like sticking a couple of photographs from a newspaper over the faces in an old master portrait and then spraying the rest with an aerosol.

7 This simple, honestly-conceived house built four square and solid; a member of a numerous family of stone houses throughout the north of England has been visually destroyed by the inappropriate application of a weak, half-timbered design, bearing no relation to its construction or to true half-timbering. About as effective as clipping a bulldog to look like a poodle.

1

2

3

4

5

6

7

Further reading

OVER A THOUSAND BOOKS have been consulted during the research for *Houses of Britain*. Most of these were difficult to find; books on house building go out of date quickly and many must have been pulped during the 1939-45 war. But there are a number of good books that have been published recently on various aspects of the subject making useful further reading. This is a selection:

English Cottages and Farmhouses (1954) by Olive Cook with photographs by Edwin Smith is a marvellous collection of black-and-white pictures, superbly printed, taken from all parts of England.

The British House, a concise Architectural History (1994) Edmund Grey, Barrie & Jenkins. Interesting history of the house and its internal period fixtures and fittings.

The Care and Conservation ot Georgian Houses (1978) Andy Davey, Bob Heath, Desmond Hodges, Mandy Ketchtin, Roy Mllne; Butterworth, 4th Ed. 1995. Mainly concerned with Edinburgh but a good practical guide to restoration procedures

The Engilah Terraced House (1982) Stefan Muthesius, Yale University Press. A useful introduction to the variety and evolution of the terraced house plan and the composition of the terrace in the town.

The English House through Seven Centuries (1968) by the same authors, is a large, useful book.

The Pattern of English Building (1972) by Alec Clinon-Taylor is a mine of information on traditional building materials.

Irish Folk Ways (1957) by Estyn Evans is one of the very few books dealing with Irish cottages.

The Thatched Houses of the Old Highlands (1953) by Colin Sinclair is a useful, short survey of the old cottages of the north of Scotland.

Three Centuries of Architectural Craftsmanship (1977) & *Period Houses and thelr Detalls* (1974) Edited Colln Amery Butterwoth (1992). Two collections of measured drawings originally published in loose format by the Architects Journal as the 'Practical Exemplar of Architecture'. Very good source for the correct details and moulding profiles for houses of this period.

Vernacular Architecture (new edition) by R W Brunskill shows a sensible method of analysing traditional buildings with excellent brief descriptions of what to look for.

English Village Homes (1936) by Sydney R Jones, is a well-illustrated and useful work, though many of the examples shown have 126 since been destroyed.

The English Farmhouse and Cottage (1961) and The House and Home (1963) both by M W Barley are two useful books, both well-detailed and illustrated.

Life in the Moorlands of North-East Yorkshire (1972) by Marie Hartley and Joan Ingilby, is a fascinating account of country life and its background; much of it applies to the rest of the country.

Building in England down to 1540 (1952) by L F Salzman is a scholarly account based on immense research.

London: The Unique City (1937) by Steen Eiler Rasmussen, a Danish architect, is still the best account of the architectural growth of the Capital.

The Care of Old Buildings Today (1972) by Donald Insall is a very complete account of current preservation methods by an architect who has enormous experience.

Cambridge Stone (1967) by Donovan Oyrcell is a useful and illuminating account of the history of the use of stone for one small area, much of which applies in principle to other places.

The English Cottage (1938) by Batsford and Fry has well selected illustrations and a great deal of useful information.

Mews Style (1998) by Sebastian Deckker has wonderful illustrations and is probably the best book on mews houses.

The Principles of Physical Geology (1964) by Arthur Holmes is an immense tome but it is an excellent place to find a complete answer about a difficult point ignored by smaller books.

The Development of English Building Construction (1916) by C F Innocent has fortunately been reprinted recently. It is an excellent account of primitive building methods, many of which were in use until the early part of this century.

A Future for the Past (1961) by Kelsall and Harris is a most useful book on the restoration of simple buildings, particularly in Scotland.

All these books are fairly easy to find; they are in public libraries, some are in print and others can be found in second-hand bookshops. Other books, too numerous to list, that can be useful bought second-hand are the many Country Life books published in the 1920s. There are lots of books on specific parts of the country published in the thirties by Batsford.

The classic books are both more difficult to find and more expensive: *A History of the English House* (1931) by Nathaniel Lloyd, early copies of *The Studio* magazine, the *RIBA Journal*, *The Building News*, Sydney Addy's *Evolution of the English House* (1898), Peate's *The Welsh House* (1944) and the much older books by Loudon, Nicholson, Paine, Ware and Palladio.

Museums

Acknowledgements

Museum of East Anglian Life
Stowmarket
Suffolk P14 1DL
Tel: Stowmarket (01449) 61 2229
www.suffolkcc.gov.uk/tourism/meal

Bunratty Castle Museum
Bunratty
Co. Clare
Eire
Tel: Limerick (00 353 61) 361 511

Highland Folk Museum
Kingussie
Inverness PH21 1JG
Tel: Kingussie (01540)661 307
www.highlandfolk.com
www.highlandfolk.com/kingussie
www.highlandfolk.com/main

Beamish
North of England Open Air Museum
Beamish
Stanley
Co. Durham OH9 0RG
Tel: Stanley (01207) 231811
www.beamishmuseum.co.uk

Museum of Welsh Life
St. Fagans
Cardiff CF5 6XB
Tel: Cardiff (01222) 569441
www.nmgw.ac.uk/mwl/index.en

Ulster Folk Museum
Cultra
Holywood
Co. Down BT1 18 OEU
Tel: 01232 428 428

Weald and Downland Open Air Museum
Singleton near Chichester
West Sussex PO18 0EU
Tel: Singleton (0124 3811) 348

The author wishes to thank, for their kindness, the many people who assisted in the photography of their houses for inclusion in this book. He would like to acknowledge the patient help and assistance given by many organisations and people: the Courtauld Institute for guidance on colour history; Alan Keeler, the designer and art director; Joanna Tanlaw for her research, and all those named in the list of contributors; also to many members of the Blue Circle Group: Bob Sobey on matters of production; Michael Greer and John Townsend on the editorial content; Jack Whalley, Jim Coldrey, Victor Hole and Geoff Hayes on advice on plastering and decoration; Tony Gladwell for his tolerant advice and help on the geological content; likewise Gren Davies on the section on colour appreciation, and Ken Brittain, Austin Edge and Shirley Coston on building matters. His thanks are due, in particular, to Peter Grondona of the Blue Circle Group, with whom the book was conceived, and who has worked with the author on it since its inception. Also to Eric Corker and Ian Bradbery for their comments on the copy; Jeremy Greenwood for guidance and advice, and Ronnie Davidson-Houston for his editing; Trudy Temkin for her editing and typography, and Rowley Atterbury of Westerham Press for guidance on printing; also to George Greer, Malcolm Kafetz, David Batterham and Philip Hicks for supplying many of the reference books and their splendid companionship and advice on photographic trips. Lastly, thanks are due to Julia Wilson for her painstaking typing and patience in producing this book; and to his wife, Willow, for her help throughout.

Index of places

Aberaeron, Dyfed, 20, 31, 116
Aberdeen, 62
Aberystwyth, Dyfed, 120
Airth, Stirlingshire, 79
Aldeburgh, Suffolk, 70, 86
Ashburton, Devon, 53
Ashton, Devon, 59
Ashwell, Hertfordshire, 56
Avebury, Wiltshire, 67, 120

Ballyvaughan, Co. Clare,37,118
Bath, Avon, 20, 60, 68, 108, 120
Bayswater, London, 116
Bealaclugga, Co. Clare,73
Bedford Square, London, 116
Beecholme Estate, London, 93
Biggleswade, Bedfordshire, 82
Bishop's Nympton, Devon,118
Blackheath, London, 102, 103
Blockley, Gloucestershire, 79
Boothby Pagnell, Lincolnshire, 73
Borrowdale, Cumbria, 74
Bourne End, Buckinghamshire, 105
Bowness, Solway, Cumbria, 65, 79
Braintree, Essex, 93
Brancaster, Norfolk, 70
Brent Eleigh, Suffolk, 108
Brighton, East Sussex, 20, 94, 98, 120
Bristol, Avon, 51
Brixton, London, 82
Burren, The, 16

Cahir, Co. Tipperary, 31
Caldbeck, Cumbria, 79
Calne, Wiltshire, 51,106, 116
Cardington, Salop, 94
Carlisle, Cumbria, 32, 67, 82, 85
Cashel, Co. Tipperary, 31,98, 116, 118
Castle Coombe, Avon, 68,98
Chancery Lane, London, 49
Chislehurst, Kent, 93
Clare, Suffolk, 98, 100
Clarecastle, Co. Clare, 31
Clifton-on-Teme, Hereford and Worcester, 49
Coggeshall, Essex, 82
Cotswolds, 13,20,28,61, 66, 68, 79, 85, 115

Crawley New Town, West Sussex, 105
Cromer, Norfolk, 74
Culross, Fife, 20, 97

Dartmoor, 73, 74
Debenham, Suffolk, 25
Didbrook, Gloucestershire, 44, 49

East Barsham Manor, Norfolk, 82
Edgware, London, 38
Edinburgh, 115
Egerton, Kent, 51
Elstead, Surrey, 80
Elterwater, Cumbria, 77
Ennis, Co. Clare,31,116

Finchley, London, 93
Fleet Street, London, 49
Folkestone, Kent, 43
Forest Row, East Sussex, 51
Framlingham, Suffolk, 49
Fyfield, Essex, 53

Giant's Causeway, Co. Antrim, 63
Glastonbury, Somerset, 118
Great Dunmow, Essex, 100
Great Yarmouth, Norfolk, 86
Greensted, Essex, 42
Groomsport, Co. Down, 98
Guildford, Surrey, 85

Haddenham, Buckinghamshire, 56
Hadleigh, Suffolk, 25
Hampstead, London, 85
Harrow, London, 49
Hayes Barton, Devon, 59
Hebrides, 73
Hemingford Grey, Cambridgeshire, 49
Henfield, West Sussex, 53
Hereford, 44
Hesket Newmarket, Cumbria, 100,113
Hull, Humberside, 80, 82
Hurstpierpoint, East Sussex, 53,85, 94

Ipswich, Suffolk, 80
Inishmurray, Co Sligo, 73

John O'Groat's, Caithness, 73
Jura, Argyll, 49

King's Lynn, Norfolk, 29, 32, 67, 79, 82, 89, 115,116
Kintbury, Berkshire, 16, 31, 82
Knockananna, Co. Limerick, 120
Knole, Kent, 110

Lake District, 63, 68, 74,85
Lavenham, Suffolk, 44
Leatherhead, Surrey, 108
Letchworth Garden City, Hertfordshire, 38
Lincoln, 110
Lismore, Co. Waterford, 20
Little Morton Hall, Cheshire, 44
Little Wenham Hall, Suffolk, 82
Liverpool, Merseyside, 51
Llanerfyl, Powys, 74
Llanfrothen, Gwynedd, 46, 106
London, 8,20, 22,24,25, 31, 35,38, 42, 46, 49,53, 67, 77, 79,82, 84, 85,89,93,98, 101, 102, 103,110, 115, 116
Lye, Hereford and Worcester, 56
Lyneham Hall, Devon, 63

Mallow, Co. Cork, 73
Mapledurham, Berkshire, 82
Marlborough, Wiltshire, 20
Melbourn, Cambridgeshire, 59
Mettingham Hall, Suffolk, 86
Milton Abbas, Dorset, 59
Milton Malbay, Co. Clare, 106
Minehead, Somerset, 55,56
Mitcham, London, 46, 89
Molesworth, Cheshire, 38
Montagu Square, London, 20
Morphany Hall, Cheshire, 51
Mortlake, London, 35

Nurstead Court, Kent, 73

Oban, Argyll, 31

Pennines, 64, 65, 68
Perth, 32, 67
Plas Newydd, Clwyd, 44

Reading,Berkshire,60,70,1(115
Regent's Park, London, 98 101
Ripon, North Yorkshire, 22
Rolvenden, Kent, 53

St Clere's Hall, Essex, 51
St David's, Dyfed, 74
St James's Square, London, 77
Salford, Greater Manchester, 94
Salisbury, Wiltshire, 70
Samlesbury, Lancashire, 77
Selworthy, Somerset, 108
Shap Fell, Cumbria, 63
Sheepwash, Hampshire, 51
Shefford, Bedfordshire, 85
Shipham, Norfolk, 59
Smarden, Kent, 53
Snowdon, Mount, 70
Snowshill, Gloucestershire, 6
South Downs, 115
South Harting, West Sussex, 77, 106
Southill, Bedfordshire, 108
Stanway, Gloucestershire, 20
Stokesay Castle, Salop, 44
Strata Florida, Dyfed, 74
Streatham, London, 53

Tayside, 118
Teapot Hall, Lincolnshire, 4
Teddington, London, 46
Tenterden, Kent, 20, 44
Thaxted, Essex, 32
Torryburn, Fife, 37
Toseland, Cambridgeshire, 4
Tower of London, 24
Tyneside, 16

Walsham-le-Willows, Suffolk 25
Weald, The, 20, 51
Welwyn Garden City, Hertfordshire, 22
West Hampstead, London, White Cliffs of Dover, 66
Winchester, Hampshire, 89
Winster, Derbyshire, 77

York, 51, 100
Youlgreave, Derbyshire, 75